BARRY LEWIS

To Irene
& Chris,

Hope you enjoy reading
these columns as much as I did
writing them. Best Wishes!

Barry Lewis

From
Brooklyn
to
Bucolic

The life of columnist Barry Lewis

Royal Fireworks Press
Unionville, New York

From Brooklyn
to
Bucolic

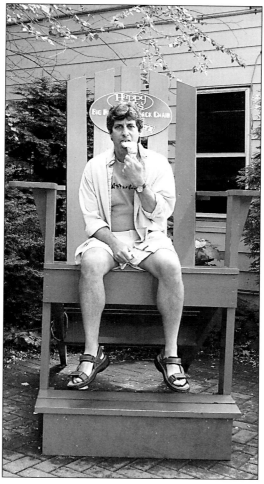

The life of columnist Barry Lewis

Royal Fireworks Press
Unionville, New York

Royal Fireworks Press

First Ave., PO Box 399

Unionville, New York 10988

(845) 726-4444

Fax (845) 726-3824

Email: mail@rfwp.com

Website: rfwp.com

ISBN: 978-0-89824-966-8

Printed and bound in the United States of America by American citizens using recycled, acid-free paper, vegtable-based inks, and environmentally-friendly cover coatings at the Royal Fireworks Printing Company of Unionville, New York.

To Sean, Daniel and Dustin, for giving me more laughs
and tears than they'll ever know.
Without them, I would have nothing to write about.

From Brooklyn to Bucolic
The Life of Columnist Barry Lewis

BARRY'S BUCOLIC LIFE AT HOME:

BARRY'S BUCOLIC LIFE IN THE COUNTRY:

BARRY TAKES A HOLIDAY:

BARRY'S MOMMA ROZ:

Barry's Life

Support, not style, matters for swimsuits

So I'm looking in men's bathing suits, and I don't like what I see. Specifically, it's what I don't see that I don't like.

I'll explain.

I went to buy a new bathing suit.

It wasn't out of desire as much as necessity. The elastic had worn out to the point that the simple task of walking to water — much less diving into a pool — would have caused me to get arrested in most states.

That's the tasteful test for guys and bathing suits. Style be damned. If it stays up, we're good for another year.

Unlike women, who take their bathing suit wearing very seriously and will buy a new one every season. This despite the fact that you will rarely see a woman in just a bathing suit. Even in water. They cover them with tees and tunics, skirts and shorts and dresses and vests. That's because they're more sensitive about their bodies.

Men should pay attention to women.

Men should be more sensitive about their bodies. Wear bulky robes all the time. Leave the Speedos to 5-year-olds.

But we don't. We're stupid.

We walk around in public places wearing the most unflattering — dare I say, bordering on the obscene — pieces of bathing material imaginable. The only thing worse would be to go around naked, and in some suits we're just about there.

Here's a good rule of thumb: You don't want to wear a bathing suit that reveals your religion.

Realizing that I have a body less like Adonis and more like an abdominal strain (caused by sucking in my chest while wearing a bathing suit), I went shopping for the more conservative look.

My wife suggested an outdoor shop that specializes in bathing suits. They had hundreds of suits from which to choose. Every one different. Solids. Stripes. Tribal tattoos. Flowers. Pictures of sunsets. Guys surfing. Guys driving. Guys driving into the sunset with a surf board.

And lots of pockets. Pockets on the inside, on the outside, with special compartments sporting zippers, snaps and Velcro. If I filled half these pockets I'd drown.

Everything I could want in a bathing suit, except more bathing suit. Inside the

Left: I picked up a hitch hiker in St. Marks Square in Venice, 2007.

suit. Where it counts. For, you know, reinforcement.

I looked in every suit. EVERY SUIT. All netless.

These must be shorts that look like suits.

"Excuse me," I asked the pretty blonde with the pierced face. "Where are your bathing suits?"

"They're all around you."

"No, those can't be bathing suits, because, well you see there's nothing inside them," I said, lowering my voice a few octaves.

She tilted her head. I wasn't sure if she was giving me a quizzical look or someone had walked in with a magnet. I pressed on.

"They don't have any support."

"Ohhh." She straightened up. The guy with the magnet must have left. "These are board shorts. Most guys have underwear under them."

Now my head was tilting.

"So, you go into the water wearing these board shorts and your underwear?"

The last time I wore anything under a bathing suit it was a diaper. That might be down the road, but for right now, I don't need any additional layers.

I told her they'd have enough extra material for the inside if they didn't waste it on suits that go past your knees.

She said the board shorts are made of a polyester material that dries fast. This way, guys can walk around with what look like shorts, so they don't have to change.

"Yeah," I said, "but they're still walking around with wet underwear."

She suggested I'd probably be more comfortable shopping for a bathing suit at a men's store in the mall.

I suggested she start selling some talcum powder so the cool dudes with the dry board shorts and wet underwear are more comfortable walking around.

July 05, 2007

Cue the Bee Gees
and push up your sleeves

I almost lost my polyester robin's-egg blue jacket.

Or should I dare say … had it stolen!

For there the evidence lay, discarded in the Good Will pile by the woman I trusted, the mother of our three children.

My wife had no problem committing to "in sickness and in health" yet thought nothing of the pain in my heart as she planned to give away the attire of my youth.

It was actually sharing floor space with my polyester white three-piece suit, complete with the polyester black shirt.

Thank God she didn't find my synthetic disco ball shirt.

The lit dance floor was my playground.

An arm here, a leg there. I stomped on toes and smacked heads, trying out the latest craze. I moved to "Staying Alive." My dance partner moved to stay out of traction.

Why not just scratch up my "Saturday Night Fever" album, shred my elephant bells and pull the elastic out of my wide clip-on rainbow suspenders?

Does she think the person who puts on the polyester robin's-egg blue jacket one day – and my polyester white three-piece suit, complete with the polyester black shirt the next – will appreciate the fine artificial material they have on?

My wife said we need the room.

"You don't wear it anymore. You haven't worn it in 20 years!"

No one's worn these clothes in 20 years, except for the swingers in white bucks and dangling jewelry who scope out Bubbies at the weekly singles extravaganza at the Boca Raton community center.

But that's getting away from the point.

"It's for the boys. They'd love to wear this stuff. I want to pass on to them my clothes. My history. Consider it my living will."

My wife and I took time out from our squabble to tend to the boys, who had hyperventilated from laughing so hard.

I say let them all laugh.

These synthetic fibers are like Twinkees and roaches. Tremendous staying power. We'll be long gone, but the bugs, cream-filled cakes and Leisure Suits will survive.

I focused on the pile.

Will these Good Will folks even know how to wear the polyester robin's-egg blue jacket?

Do they have the appropriate dress T-shirt?

Will they know to pull up the sleeves to show off that sprayed on Florida tan?

Will they know not to shave?

Because if you wear the jacket, you can't shave. Or you can't look like you just shaved. Day or night these "Miami Vice" guys always had that cool-looking 5 o'clock shadow.

No matter how hard I tried getting the 5 o'clock shadow, I always ended up with a 3:30 stubble or 9:30 need a shave look.

That's a lot to remember: No sleeves, no shave and no socks.

Yea, no socks.

If you're gonna wear the polyester robin's-egg blue jacket, don't you dare put on a pair of socks.

What?

You think Crockett and Tubbs worried about smelly, sweaty feet in a pair of leather shoes while walking the Miami streets in the middle of summer?

(No truth to the rumor that producers were thinking of a attracting an older audience with a spin-off staring Abe Vigoda called Miami Beach Bunions).

Oh, to be young, shaveless and sockless in my polyester robin's-egg blue jacket with the sleeves pulled up. Hiding behind dark shades, a warm breeze kicking up my hair as I ride the wake in a motor boat. The musical sounds of Jan Hammer fill the air.

All right, the water was Swan Lake, the ripples were from the oars of our rowboat and the only sound you heard were summer guests complaining about the food.

Sure, you're laughing now.

Yea, like you didn't wear this?

You want me to send my wife over and rummage through your closet to find those prize pieces of pastel pink polyester?

Fess up. Let me know what you've got hidden away. Stuff you could never part with. Nothing retro. It's got to be real.

Or as real as polyester could pretend to be.

May 01, 2003

Forget Lauer!
I am master of my dome mane

L ook what Matt Lauer has me doing.

I look like the front man for the '80s rock band Twisted Sister. Lead singer Dee Snyder and I could be twins.

It's my backlash to Matt Lauer and his haircut.

I hate that haircut.

Hey, it's nice to see a pleasant-looking face on TV in the morning, especially when the alternative is staring right back at me in the mirror.

But all that changed when Lauer fell asleep in the barber chair.

My problem with Mr. Morning Man starts and stops at his scalp, which you can see a lot more of these days.

I go to bed Sunday night, comfortable in the knowledge that I am the master of my dome mane. Only to wake up the next morning and find the most watched man in America has set the grooming agenda for the mature male with his hideous buzz cut.

His close crop 'do has put undo pressure on those of us still coming to grips with a more pronounced forehead.

Right or wrong, the impact of the Lauer look extends far beyond Rockefeller Plaza.

Women view the short, spunky Lauer look as the hot hairstyle for the middle-aged man. I've read how it has fostered a revival of the aging hotties, with Lauer

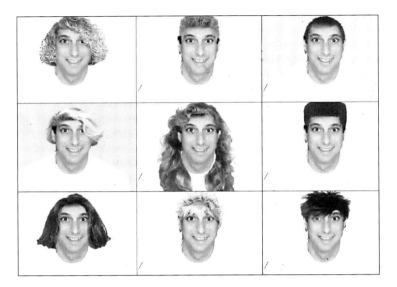

following in the salon seat of Pacino, Gere and Clooney.

I suppose if you already have a reputation as a hottie, women wouldn't give a hoot if you woke up one day and decided to put hay on your head.

"Gee Richard Gere … that's a great head of hay you have on. You wear it so natural. Alfalfa brings out the blue in your eyes."

Back on Earth, they rest of us mortals get poked and prodded by wives who coax themselves into believing – maybe praying – that a buzz to our scalp will turn us into an aging hottie.

If that's all it took, I would have shaved every hair off my body. Instead, we get these not-so-subtle grooming suggestions.

"See …. Matt Lauer got his hair cut. And it looks nice. Why don't you?"

Sure it looks nice, matched with a blue suit, perfect lights and professional makeup artists.

Stick him in the bathroom, in underwear and a day's stubble and suddenly this hottie ain't too hot.

The rage over his roots has me ready to pull mine out.

I saw Matt's chopped coif as a sign of folic failure.

A thin-skinned man unable to face his thinning head-on.

Couldn't stand the heat, huh Lauer?

Well, I'm not ready to give the locks without a fight.

Growing up, it was all about the hair. Lots of hair. Somewhere amid my hair there was a face. And braces. I looked like hairy barbed wire.

It took me nearly 30 years to come to the realization that haircuts should come with a bit more regularity than oil changes.

When I did sit in the chair, it was more about trimming than actual cutting.

Like Lauer, I was also hearing the whispers at the salon.

But unlike the showbiz hotshots, I didn't succumb to the scissors, but compromised with the clippers.

At age 40 I decided it was time to be bold. To make a statement. To set a trend.

"OK, Gina," I said to my hairdresser at Creative Cutters in Ellenville, "let's see the ears." At long last I decided to go above the lobes.

I considered it a coming-of-age moment, a milestone of maturity, a new look for the new millennium.

Gina just said it's about time.

We left the ever-increasing gray, which I credit to the three boys. Like the rings of an old tree, the gray bore out my years of fatherhood.

But the buzz never touched the scalp.

Maybe in another 30 years it will.

I might be ready for a clean, close crop. By then the alternatives might be comb-overs, hairpieces or plugs.

Matt, you can't hide behind the buzz.

Be a man, face the truth. Or at least get yourself a great '80s wig.

October 03, 2002

Rose-colored glasses morph to half-frames

Despite tying my wrists to my ankles and trying to walk with my back straight, I'm ready to admit I can't get my arms to grow any longer. I'm also ready to admit that I'm having a hard time reading what I write on the computer screen (which some might suggest is a good thing, but that's a topic for another day).

And I'm ready to admit there's nothing wrong with the picture on my television screen (although I won't admit this to my wife, and I'm still bucking for one of those floor-to-ceiling wide-screen models).

So, I decided to come clean and give up my vanity for my vision.

I broke down and got glasses.

For folks older and much wiser than me, this is a no-brainer.

You can't see – you get glasses.

I can rationalize the fact that your eyes start to go as you keep going.

But what I've had a hard time accepting is that at 44, I've become just another baby boomer who's fallen victim to the laws of basic physiology.

As America's most influential generation, we were witness to everything from Vietnam and Woodstock to the fall of the Berlin Wall and the rise of the Internet.

For image-conscious folks who swore we'd never grow old and were willing to be nipped and tucked and lifted and plucked and have fat sucked out and jell stuffed in – being far-sighted is like a kick in the shins.

Not that I'm completely vain about getting old. For one thing, I've left in the gray.

I consider those light streaks in my hair as battle scars – signs of valor that I would never consider covering with a hat or erasing with some funky coloring formula.

I could control the hair.

But I'm trying to figure out when it was that I could no longer read the date on the face of my watch.

There was also a time when reading a menu was as easy as opening it. Now I practically have to ask my wife to hold it up.

Still, I held out hope I was simply suffering from vision fatigue and not visual frailty when the eye doctor had me look into a machine and read him the chart.

Piece of cake.

Thanks doc, I'm cured.

"Now read it using just the other eye."

Suddenly the letters chart looked just like the date on the face of my watch. Blurry.

He called it presbyopia, a fancy word for when the lens of the eye becomes thicker and less flexible. Boy, doesn't that describe old age.

He said not to worry. It happens to everyone as they age. I just need reading glasses.

Like that's comforting? As if I really care about the other 76 million baby boomers who have found, or soon will, that they can't get their arms any longer and will also need to deal with presbyopia?

With the reality of needing proper prescriptive eyewear, I traded in my rose-colored glasses for a pair of half-frames.

Or did I want bifocals, trifocals and multifocals? Was I looking for something in an Ashleigh Banfield, maybe something sassy with a matching cord or was I a gunmetal type of guy?

Another option was a three-piece plastic rimless model in crystal.

For a second I wondered if I was getting glasses, a suit or dinnerware.

I also could get eye surgery and have a laser shot into my eye and change its shape. Or I could try conductive keratoplasty, a new procedure where a tiny instrument sends radio waves on the outer cornea, increasing its curvature.

I might have lost some of my vision, but not my sanity. I went with the half-frames.

But the glasses seemed cockeyed. The eye doctor said no problem … I just have uneven ears.

Great. My eyes are going and my ears are uneven. I wanted to get out of the place before he decided to test any other part of my body.

So I did. Now I get those wonderful backhanded complements.

My wife told me I look smarter. Give that a chance to sink in for a minute. My boys said I look like grandpa.

I'll show them.

I'll stick around another 30 years to watch them try to stretch their arms.

If I can see them.

October 21, 2004

That Saul guy
really kneaded me

I'm lying on a table with nothing on but my underwear, paying some guy a decent chunk of change to pour oil, heated at 120 degrees, all over my body. And as my skin begins to take on the shiny color of a newly fried onion ring, I try to muffle my whimpers from this most unusual form of pain.

He then proceeds to carefully place piping hot rocks on top of the oil.

"Are the rocks and oil too hot?" asks my male masseur, who seems ready to start roasting marshmallows from the heat coming off my chest.

It was then that I thought back to the reassuring comments made by my wife just moments before:

"A massage will make you feel like a new person."

Of course I would feel like a new person. And in 45 minutes, I'd have the skin grafts to prove it.

I'll be honest, I've never really been a massage type of guy.

Having a person I'd never met push his hands across my skin to work out my kinks and knots – whether the kinks and knots wanted to get worked out or not – just doesn't seem that relaxing.

But when we recently took our first cruise, my wife said there's no better way to start a vacation on a boat than to get an Aroma Stone Therapy massage.

Really? I thought lounging by the pool with a funny-sounding drink and getting up only to eat my way through the buffet was a pretty good start.

Then she showed me pictures of men lying on their stomachs, practically comatose but with Cheshire smiles, as soft female hands caressed their upper backs.

I imagined the gentle touch from the blond-haired Inga from Sweden, who would leave me renewed and refreshed. Instead, I got a pounding from the hairy-knuckled Saul from the island of Malta, who in a previous life was the activities director at the Spanish Inquisition.

The man took pleasure watching my teardrops sizzle as they hit my burning chest.

Feel like a new person?

I was feeling like a spare rib on the grill waiting for Saul of Malta to pour on the barbecue sauce.

My only other thought: How much was I supposed to tip Saul for what I swore to myself would be a once-in-a-lifetime torture? I mean treatment.

Then again, what's a little pain – OK, a lot of pain – when the payoff is having volcanic basalt stones, anointed with hot exotic island flower body oil, rubbed across my skin?

And how did I know these were basalt stones and exotic island flower oil – and not some smooth rocks from the Hudson and baby oil from Eckerd?

Because that's what Saul told me, as he pushed the stones across my back, allowing me to experience an odd combination of hot oil and hairy knuckles.

As I was in a somewhat vulnerable position, it just didn't seem like the right time to question the man's belief in the ancient Polynesian philosophy of therapy.

He told me these stones would unblock any stagnant energy, melt away pain and stress, restore my equilibrium and allow me to drift in a world of pure bliss.

Saul stressed that for my inner self to emerge beyond this Aroma Stone Therapy session, I would need to commit to a weekly hot bath of cleansing and detoxifying, have exotic lime and ginger salt rubbed into my joints and apply a heated seaweed mask at least twice a month.

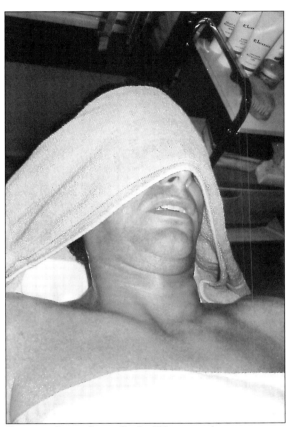

I'm pretending to sleep so Saul will leave me alone.

And I might want to consider putting my feet in warm milk.

As the session ended, I did feel rejuvenated, all my pain and stress having melted away … up until I found out just how expensive it is to drift in a world of bliss.

I'm too embarrassed to say how much it cost, but I could have taken my wife, Inga and Saul out to a pretty fancy restaurant instead.

I thanked Saul and told him that if I could make do without having HBO, I certainly could live with blocked energy and an unbalanced equilibrium.

But I might try the milk – after it cools down.

August 11, 2005

Barry's Boys

Dustin, Daniel and Sean in Lake George, 2002.

DANIEL JOSEPH SMYTHE
2008

Javelin drives home point about boys

My son calls to tell me he accidentally impaled himself with his own javelin.

He didn't throw the javelin and impale someone else. Nor did someone throw the javelin into him.

No, he got himself with the tail end of his javelin.

I'll explain it all in just a second, but let me assure you he's perfectly fine. Really.

Are you wondering why I'd share such news?

Timing.

Less than an hour before receiving that call from my son – remember, he's perfectly fine – I received an email called "Raising Boys."

It was one of those junk e-mails people like to pass around. You know the kind. Someone sharing a joke, a video or a touchy-feely phrase of spiritual renewal.

They want you to pass it on to 10 people, who are asked to pass it on to 10 more people. Pretty soon, you're exchanging touchy-feely messages from strangers you wouldn't talk to on a checkout line.

This particular e-mail listed 25 ways boys manage to get themselves in the darnedest situations.

I'm not talking about how boys manage to get so dirty.

More like how boys will experiment mixing Clorox and brake fluid.

How boys experiment with pool filters and Jell-O.

How boys experiment on not-so-nice things to the pet cat.

Supposedly, this originated from an anonymous mother in Austin, Texas, on things she learned from her boys.

My guess is that the woman chooses to remain anonymous because she fears retaliation from either the Austin Department of Social Services, her boys or the pet cat.

I read it. Cute. But nothing new to me.

I've got my own list, thanks to twin sons who will turn 18 in less than a month. My oldest son will be 21.

I've seen it all. Heard it all.

I don't need no stinkin' list to tell me about the trouble boys are capable of getting into.

I remember thinking, that's all behind me.

That's just about the time my son calls to tell me about this unusual thing that happened while he was practicing throwing a javelin during track.

He was punctured by his own javelin.

I bet that mom in Austin, Texas, never thought to include self-inflicted wound from a javelin on her list.

Being the conscientious parent, I ask, "Are you OK?"

Being a teenager, he replies, "Yeah, I guess, except I got a little hole on my side that's red and sort of oozing. Are you gonna bring home pizza?"

Let me assure you that he's perfectly fine. Really.

Let me also assure you that no member of the Flying Wallendas could have managed this gravity-defying feat.

I had him show it to me in slow-motion as we waited in the hospital emergency room.

He runs with the javelin and throws it a short way, but in the process his feet get a bit tangled and he stumbles and falls onto the pointed tail of the javelin. He's fine. Really.

For years, we've been telling the boys to be careful: Don't run around in the house with a sharp object! Someone will get hurt! You'll poke your eye out! Who knew the same rules applied for kids practicing outside on a track?

What was I supposed to tell him? Don't run outside with a javelin? Throw it and run the opposite way?

Waiting several hours for the CAT scan – just a precaution – gave me time to think about that boys' list. It's true: The stuff they attempt, it ages us.

You warn them to be careful, be smart, do the right thing. You don't want to hover and hound them and control every action and reaction – but you don't want to see them get hurt.

You can't predict the next crisis. And there will be a next crisis.

It's the balancing act that doesn't end. It only evolves with time.

We worried when they were babies and boys and now teens. We'll worry next month when they want to go to the graduation party and in the fall when they're in college.

And we'll still worry when our boys become men and husbands and fathers.

My son's perfectly fine. Really.

But I need to contact that woman in Austin, Texas. I've got something for her list.

June 23, 2006

At 16, he's pondering fine cuisine

'What's the catch of the day?"

Our waiter Carl is about to open his mouth, unaware of the dangers that will fall upon him if he answers. I shoot him a glance that would stop traffic.

"Carl ... can you give us a minute? I don't think we're ready to order just yet."

I turn to our 16-year-old, once again amazed by his culinary inquisitiveness at the expense of my wallet. With a forced smile and clenched teeth, I ask, "what are you doing?"

"I wanna know what's the catch of the day."

"But we're in a diner," I explain, hoping to find the switch that might shed some light in his still-maturing mind. "Are we near the ocean or any large body of water? Pick something else."

So while the wife and I stick with the chicken sandwich that comes with fries, our oldest informs us he's undecided between the rib eye steak and the clam and shrimp marinara.

But he will start with a some steamed clams.

At this point I'm undecided if he's walking home.

He religiously bases orders not on what his taste buds fancy, but on how many vowels and zeros are on a menu. I'm not suggesting our growing boy down a leafy salad, but shouldn't there be some rule about ordering an entrée you cannot pronounce?

How does a kid who chooses Cocoa Puffs and macaroni and cheese at home question if "Zuppa diPesce" includes calamari or if "Penne à la Vodka" is made with real fresh tomatoes? Not that he would know a calamari from a scungilli, but at such prices, it's gotta be good.

No matter where we go, he scours the menu in search of those mightiest of creatures, the allusive surf-n-turf, beef-n-reef or seafood combo, a meal fit for a king, but hardly for a teen who's never seen a credit card statement.

Sometimes it's worth letting him order just to see his reaction to a serving of shrimp and lobster sauce. Not exactly what he had in mind.

At times we cheat, pulling into a Ponderosa and telling the boys to go crazy.

"You mean we can take anything up there?"

"Anything. Pile it on. You can even have seconds. But make room for dessert. You can make your own."

Long gone are the days when we could safely go to a restaurant and ask, without any arguments from the peanut gallery, to see the children's menu.

We never questioned how they could charge $2.50 for peanut butter and jelly, knowing it came with a drink, ice cream and enough crayons and crackers to keep any child occupied.

But as the boys got older, ordering from the "children's menu" was as embarrassing to them as training wheels and holding hands while crossing the street. Youngsters see the "children's menu" as questioning their maturity. It meant they were children ... limited to a burger, spaghetti or chicken fingers. The fact that they were children who wanted a burger, spaghetti or chicken fingers was irrelevant.

The choice had been made for them.

Our little man would pout, "only babies order from the children's menu."

What followed was my moment of weakness. I uttered the words that would haunt me the rest of my life. "Honey, he's a big boy. Let him order what he wants."

And with that, tuna fish became "Grilled Yellowfin Tuna Steak with Artichoke-Potato Pancakes, topped in a Zinfandel Sauce."

It adds up. Jumbo shrimp scampi, ziti boscaola or pan-roasted breast of moulard duck. There's just no shortcuts.

What'ya say kids. This weekend ... Ponderosa.

August 23, 2001

Sean, my proud EMT.

Pre-law, pre-life ... same thing

My son calls from college Tells us he wants to be a doctor.
My son, the doctor. Isn't that great news?
Who wouldn't want their child to be a doctor?

Says he's been giving it serious thought.

But he wants to know if his credits will transfer.

A conscientious doctor.

"Well, let's see," I reply, trying to remain upbeat, not wanting to discourage the lad, but still feeling the need to address some of the impediments that may – and I stress just may – lie ahead.

"You're majoring in diesel engineering ... with an emphasis on industrial hydraulics and combustible engines," I say, carefully backing in.

"I'm not sure if the credits will hold up, but these classes will certainly get you a med school interview. They love diversity."

Even I was believing this.

"I bet you'd be the only doctor who could disembowel someone's crankshaft and large intestines. Maybe at the same time. And you do have your own welding helmet."

We had that talk back in August.

Before he had all his books.

Before he had taken all his classes.

By September he had voluntarily given up medicine.

So much for free health care.

To tell you the truth, I'm less surprised that he's reconsidered pre-med and just glad he hasn't changed his major to Fundamentals in Paint Ball, with a minor in CD Burning.

Should any of us be shocked that our children might be having second thoughts about what they want to do for the rest of their lives?

How many of us have stayed the course?

The average American makes about four different career changes.

And more than 80 percent of workers are not in a career directly related to their college major.

Toll-taking is an honorable profession; I'm just not sure it takes four years of study.

Selecting a major is the first real decision a teenager makes, right between deciding what color tux to wear to the prom and which body part to pierce first.

College students are more likely to change their majors than they will their bed sheets. Certainly at a greater rate.

The problem is they have too many options.

We've got them worrying if their interests, abilities and values will match up with their majors and minors and internships and post-graduate studies – can they do it in two years? Four years? Eight years?

All the time wondering, is this what they want to do for the REST OF THEIR LIVES?

When all they're trying to figure out is what poster to put in their dorm room and which meal plan to choose.

How can you overload information on a group that can't function on less that 23 hours of sleep each night and day.

I say let's get rid of some majors.

Start with the humanities.

And anything that begins with "Introduction to ... " or "Fundamentals of ... "

And any major that ends with "ogy"

That means no entomology, mycology and enology. Look up enology and you'd say, "Hey, I paid four years for that?"

Should any parent be expected to pay for a major they can't pronounce? Or one that they must have explained to them?

I've got a cousin who majored in environmental interpretation.

His parents would boast all the time. "Our Stevie is an environmental interpreter" – as if the kid worked in the United Nations.

He cut grass and pruned trees.

So why not say he learned to cut grass and prune trees.

All of which reminds me of that line in "Animal House" where Otter says he's pre-law, but his friend Boone thought he was pre-med. Says Otter, "Same difference."

Last week my son called from college.

Tells us he now wants to be a teacher.

My son, the teacher.

I told him he can be whatever he wants to be. Just study hard and be happy.

And hold on to the welding helmet.

March 11, 2004

MapQuest is fine, but using the map puts you in control

It was just after 11 at night when I got an urgent phone call from my son, who was leaving downtown Albany after a concert at the Pepsi Arena.

"Do I make a left or a right?"

It's amazing. I've been talking to the kid for more than 20 years, and he can still start a conversation that not only catches me completely off guard, but is without any reference to anything we've ever spoken about before.

Not wanting to be difficult, I followed with my own question that I thought might help both of us move things along:

"I don't know, where do you want to go?"

"I need to get on the Thruway!"

"Where are you now?"

"I'm pulling out of the parking garage! Left or right?"

"How would I know left or right? I don't know what street you're on. It could be one-way. Where's the parking garage? Pull over and get out a map!"

Suddenly we had silence. Then, a rare admission from my all-knowing son that maybe, just possibly, by some cosmic freak of nature, Dad might be on to something.

A map. Folded-up pieces of paper with squiggly lines in various colors with names and numbers going in all different ways. It fits neatly into the glove box, never needing to see the light of day.

But it can be opened and the squiggly lines, once thought to be abstract designs with no direction, will magically lead any lost soul to the place they need to go.

And so it was, until a new generation deemed these handy papers with the squiggly lines to be as ancient as trying to navigate via the stars and no longer necessary in the age of computer technology.

Why map when you can MapQuest?

It's as simple as making toast. Keyboard your coordinates, wait and print. Sure, you're still dealing with paper, but it's only a sheet or two. No need to unfold that Chinese puzzle of a map.

So why not MapQuest?

I'll give you why not.

So you can get wherever you need to get to in less time and travel fewer miles.

Oh, MapQuest will figure out distances, estimate time of travel and plot out routes.

It'll show me the bend in the road, the fork in the road and even the road less traveled. But it won't show me the optional road. Or the road I might want to consider if the recommended road is suddenly closed. Or the road I might need to take if I inadvertently take the wrong road.

For 25 years, I've driven into Brooklyn to see my mom. Not as often as she'd like, but that's another story. I've got what I consider a direct route. And an alternate if the Palisades is flooded, an alternate if the Brooklyn Bridge is clogged, an alternate if the United Nations is in session. I can avoid the East or West side.

Just for fun, I asked MapQuest for directions.

They've got me taking 35 different steps traveling on more than a dozen different roads and highways, including six interstates, three tunnels and a bridge, and paying half-a-dozen tolls in two states. And no options.

I keep looking at the directions, and the only thing I'm sure of is making a right out of my driveway.

How did we all get around before MapQuest, GPS Locator and Google Satellite?

First time I ever drove into the city, I sat with my dad and an AAA map. He told me how to get to the George Washington Bridge. Once on it, he said just stay in the second-to-right-hand lane. No turns. It'll put you on to the FDR Drive. That'll put you on the Brooklyn Bridge.

MapQuest doesn't put you anywhere.

Stage 10 tells you to: Merge onto NJ-17 S via EXIT 163 on the LEFT toward RT-4/PARAMUS/G WASHINGTON BRIDGE for 1.6 miles.

By the time you read that, you've gone past the merge for NJ-17 S and you'll have to get off at the next exit and pull out the old AAA map to get back on the bridge.

My son? After a few more pleasantries, I pulled out a map and put him on the NY State Thruway. We bypassed Jersey.

February 09, 2006

I got a call from my son's pants

The phone rang Saturday.
"Hello?"
"Shwish … shwish … shwish … shwish."
"Hello?"
"Shwish … shwish … shwish … shwish."
"HELLO!!!!"

It sounded like I was getting an obscene phone call from a pair of corduroy pants.

"Shwish … shwish … shwish …"

It was a pair of pants. But I could also hear some noise in the background.

There were people talking. And I could make out one of the voices.

It was my son, the college student, multitasking.

He had somehow managed to walk, talk and have his cell phone call us on the weekend.

I was impressed. With his cell phone.

It had managed to do on its own what we've been trying to get him to do on his own for a year.

For the next two hours, my wife and I were joined at the hip with our son, tagging along as he walked the campus grounds, as he chewed loudly in the cafeteria, as he joked with friends and returned to his dorm room to see what his roommate was doing.

My wife suggested I try yelling his name into the receiver. Maybe he'd hear me and realize his phone was on.

Maybe.

Or maybe the other kids would begin to wonder why they could hear a man yelling out of his front pocket.

When yelling his name didn't work, I tried some show tunes. Then I belted out that Carpenters' classic, "Close to You."

My wife thought that was a nice touch.

The dog was thrilled when I stopped singing.

I even tried some subliminal messages. Maybe he'd hear a command, not know where it was coming from, but suddenly respond.

"DON'T GET A TATTOO … STUDY HARD … BE A DOCTOR … DON'T GET A TATTOO… STUDY HARD … BE A DOCTOR!"

I don't know if he actually heard me sing, had an itch or just needed some change, but we were soon disconnected.

Still, it was a great visit – the longest we've spent together in a while without getting into an argument.

I suspect the call will eat into his roaming charges – of which we pay.

Talking to our college son through his pants pocket might seem a bit cold and distant, but I consider our conversation, however muffled and one-sided, a step up from our occasional text message conversation.

Every time I get one of those cryptic forms of communication I'm usually left staring at my cell phone, asking it if I can buy a vowel.

It reminded me of my own bizarre quickie conversations I had with my parents when I made the trek back to college.

This was back in the OLD days, when the only person I knew who had a mobile telephone was Maxwell Smart.

Back in the days when pay phones were the only phone-away-from-home phones.

As I bundled up for my three-hour trip north to good old Freezyabuttoff U., my concerned parents would look me in the eye and with much warmth tell me:

"Don't forget to give us a dummy call."

Just think, there's an entire generation missing out on making the dummy call.

The idea was to use a pay phone, put no money in it but dial the operator.

I would then give the unsuspecting operator my home phone number and tell her I wanted to make a collect call to Barry Lewis.

And I would only accept to pay for the call if Barry Lewis was there to take the call.

Phone rings. My parents answer.

"Hello, this is the operator. I have a collect call for a Barry Lewis. Is Mr. Lewis there?"

My parents would say no, the phone line would go dead, but the "dummy call" signal would be received.

They knew I made it back to college.

But I'd rather hear my son's voice – even if it's through his pocket.

So a call from his pants?

I'll gladly accept the charges.

February 24, 2005

Daniel on the Tri-Valley sidelines.

Parents captive to the closing of another season

If only they let the parents of high school athletes call time-out. Maybe then we could keep our kids out on the football field just a little bit longer. So we could watch them try to leg out a few more yards on a run up the middle, pass for another first down and make a tackle at the line of scrimmage.

Anything to keep the season going.

Who's going to mind? The kids still want to play. The cheerleaders are yelling. The field's already marked.

You're telling me that four years are up? Just like that?

To tell you the truth, I don't care so much about the yards, the downs and the tackles.

Oh, I wanted to see my son's team win that last game in the worst way. They're a great bunch of kids who just play their hearts out. Never give up.

But the tears I saw filling up the reddening eyes of parents, coaches and players when the ref blew that last whistle had less to do with the Bears losing to the Bulldogs and everything to do with the fact that the years these kids had been together as teammates had just ended.

There's a pain in losing, and I don't know anyone who likes it.

The responsible parents and the smart coaches make sure kids understand that you win and lose. That's what comes with playing these games.

The responsible parent in me knew the game was lost long before that last whistle. The impractical parent in me, the one who wishes he could keep his kid from ever feeling pain or disappointment, was willing to deal with the devil to cheat time, like some "Twilight Zone" episode.

Anything to keep from seeing my son walk off that football field for the last time, holding at his side that blue helmet he felt so proud to wear. I watched the scoreboard clock wind its way down, moving with the kind of speed that leaves you wondering where the time has gone.

I'd say it was a guy thing, but I know too many football moms who swelled with as much pride as the dads standing next to them when they first caught a glimpse of their sons in that room-to-grow-into uniform.

Remember when they had to keep tucking it in so they wouldn't trip over it? Then they put on the shoulder pads and the helmet, and you wondered what happened to your kid. Where did he disappear to?

There's got to be a way to stop the clock.

Not because it would mean more playing time for my son. Not really.

The grass stains on his uniform come from the pre-game and halftime warm-ups. Some players start. Some stand on the sidelines.

That's where he's been most of these last four years. On the sidelines. Cheering on his classmates, his teammates, his friends. He loved it.

That doesn't mean he wouldn't want to play more.

You don't practice for hours wearing pads under the summer sun and watch and wait and wait in the late fall frost without wanting to join your teammates and have fun on the field.

Maybe some day they'll figure out a way to stick a line on a resume that tells how a 17-year-old trained for years for those precious opportunities he knew in his heart would be limited at best.

How he would never think of complaining to a coach for more playing time or hold back in a practice because, hey, what does it matter, I won't get to play.

How he never lost the pride in putting on that uniform. Nor did his enthusiasm to cheer on his teammates ever waver.

Stop the clock.

Not because some parents are trying to keep alive their own high school glory days – living vicariously through their kids' own heroics. And not because a bunch of kids from one rural end of Sullivan County sandwiched between farms and the Delaware River was about to beat a bunch of kids from the other rural end of the county squeezed between farms and the Neversink Reservoir.

No one could stop the clock. The board showed a couple of zeros, the ref blew the whistle, and both teams shook hands and walked off the field.

I wiped my eyes and told my son, "Good game."

November 10, 2005

Squirrel recipe is a wild game

'**S**hould I keep stirring the squirrel?"
        You hear that in your house and suddenly the Taliban and terrorism just don't seem that big a deal.

I bet even bin Laden, all the Mrs. bin Ladens and all the little bin Ladens in their little double-wide cave don't have to worry about adding too much salt to the squirrel stew.

But there was the 16-year-old, our own Davey Crockett, king of the wild frontier, peeling the potatoes and chopping the onions, mixing just the right seasonings to add some spice and life – well at least spice – to his prize catch.

And there was not just one, but three catches, all cleaned and skinned, simmering in a pot that I vowed never to use again.

"Should I dish you up some squirrel?"

"Just keep stirring," I yell, wondering if the thing still had the nut in its month.

My iron chef must have a cast-iron stomach if he planned to eat what he proudly described as the "other white meat."

I think he needs to add a couple more "others" in there before we can call it meat.

But he was going by the book.

The "Wild Game Cook Book."

Dozens and dozens of mouth-watering wild meat recipes, not from the kitchen of Betty Crocker, but the Silica Volunteer Fire Department in Silica, Minn.

It's the kind of community where friends have friends over for dinner. Literally.

You think Martha Stewart has an imagination? You'll never find any caribou on her parchment paper. Beaver tail beans. Not a good thing.

Hey, I like good steak as much as the next person. Roast duck, beautiful. Baby back ribs, heaven.

Sean with his prize catch.

I just draw the line on anything that might someday end up under my Goodyear tires.

That's not a problem for the "Wild Game Cook Book," that includes recipes for headcheese without the head, moose meat fondue (chocolate optional) and the always popular gameburger casserole, easy to make because the ground meat from any game animal will do. Let your imagination run wild and have some fun.

With these folks, there's no telling what you may find, or what they might decide to add, to the potluck casserole.

I'd call it the good-luck casserole.

Watching your calories but having a hard time cutting back on the raccoon? Just can't say "no" to a second-helping of turtle pie?

There's weight watchers' chili and chop suey. Just one pound of venison is all you'll need.

As with any responsible cook book, there are advisories.

When cooking beaver, muskrat or porcupine, "be sure the animal is completely defatted." You want to "use only young beaver" when making beaver tail and please, "don't forget to remove the scent glands" when broiling your skunk.

Like French food, the book notes that a porcupine tastes better than he looks.

Which brings us back to the squirrels, which to be honest, didn't look that bad, floating around between the potatoes and veggies.

If I didn't know better, I would have sworn we were having some funky looking chicken.

You know, if you're careful pulling out the porcupine needles, they'd make perfect sticks when serving elk-kebob.

It's a good thing.

November 08, 2001

Barry and Bonnie

An embarrassment of dishes, and muffin tins, and spice racks

My boys can rest easy. Thanks to their mom, they'll never need to buy themselves any drinking cups, dinner plates or silverware as long as they live. Wherever they might live.

But that's not all.

They won't need to buy coffee mugs, bowls or cooking utensils. They're also good for various size spatulas, colanders and those big containers to make themselves punch, lemonade or iced tea. Heck, we have enough containers put away so all three of them can each make themselves punch, lemonade AND iced tea, all at the same time.

Wherever they might live.

Everyone likes to put away a couple of things for the kids when they eventually move into their own place. Make things easier for them. Help them get a jump on domestic life — if they want our help or not.

So it's not that uncommon for moms of teenage sons to squirrel away a few things. Just to get started. With love from mom.

But after 20 years, my wife has managed to stock pile enough pieces of kitchenware to create our own little Bed Bath & Beyond in attic.

We're not rushing the boys out. God knows we still need somebody to mow the lawn, take the trash to the dump and walk the dog at night. My only fear is that when they decide to go — they may not want to take their kitchen supplies with them. Not that I blame them.

The reason why so much of this stuff is available to them is because it's no longer of need to us. And in many cases it never was needed.

"What if the boys don't want this stuff," I ask my wife as she sends me to the attic to restock our supplies.

"It'll be for their apartment."

"What if they don't have the room?"

"They'll find the room," she says. "Or they could leave some of it here until they have the room."

Thing is we have a house and we still don't have the room. And we don't want this stuff.

Last week I had to reshuffle the fondue kit and the three-piece wok set, complete with cookbook, so I could make room for a multitier, space-eating thing that looks like one of those Star Wars ships.

Left: Bonnie's winning in the battle of the Leaning Tower of Pisa, 2007.

You know what it does? It dries and shrivels up your food. I didn't even know they sell things to shrivel food. That's the way my mom always cooked for us.

I ask you, if you really want shriveled food, wouldn't you just buy it shriveled instead of wasting time waiting for some machine to do the shriveling?

We got the shriveled food thing about 15 years ago as a well-meaning gift. Guess they thought we like to eat shriveled food. We didn't use it once. What a surprise.

Did we throw it out? Give it to the United Way?

Nope, I put it on aisle 12 in the attic, between the shoe boxes of baby pictures, a set of crutches and the bedroom window screen that I swear one day I'll get fixed.

I'm sure the boys must be asking, what, no kitchen appliances?

Not to worry guys, your mom has taken care of that. Toasters. Food processors. Microwaves. You can even pick out the color. And everyone's getting a spice rack. Whether you want one or not.

How about a toaster over? A blender? A set of steak knives? How many are in our set?

How many do you need?

Thing is, I could live with an attic full of kitchen hand-me-downs. I'd hate to see the boys go out and buy themselves a can opener when we've got a couple of electric ones ready to be plugged in.

And can anyone ever have enough muffin tins?

Problem is, we're not just filling the attic.

The Ma Lewis discount department store and home storage facility has recently expanded its operations.

We're now running a furniture store out of the basement.

I'm not talking about holding on to a crib or a stroller for the future grandkids. Yea, we're doing that, too.

I mean a showroom of couches, chairs, end tables, lamps, rugs and enough seat cushions to fill the loge level at Shea. Can I interest you in a love seat?

I'm hoping she'll consider running a Labor Day sale so I could get the car in before winter.

Until then we'll just back up the fork lift and squeeze in a few more pieces. And I suppose there's always room in the attic for another casserole dish.

But if your looking for a unique housewarming or anniversary gift, left me know. I've got this great looking thing that'll dry your food. And I'll throw in a spice rack.

May 17, 2007

Mom sends freshman off with full nest

Our two-car caravan made the trip to college, full of clothes and bedding, soaps and school supplies, anticipation and trepidation. We even managed to squeeze a healthy dose of anxiety next to the television, microwave popcorn and packets of Ramen noodles.

We were nervous. My son feared getting all 8 a.m. classes, sadistic professors and a roommate who had an appetite like Hannibal Lecter.

My wife worried if her oldest son had packed enough clothes, enough food and enough items for personal hygiene. I worried about fitting everything into his room.

And that his roommate didn't have an appetite like Hannibal Lecter.

I've come to the conclusion that getting my son into college was easy.

But getting everything my son owns – and that his mom thinks he really needs – into his college dorm room was a bit more challenging.

But not just what his mom thinks.

What all moms think.

We pull up to good old Payuntilyoudrop U, and I see families unloading 18-wheelers with more appliances than a Sears warehouse.

And those were the commuting students.

I thought it was touching to see one dad cry, until I realized he just found out he had to take the stairs to reach the elevator.

I'm no Einstein, but I can do basic math: two guys + two beds + two desks + two dressers + two closets divided by a 10 x 10 foot space = little room for anything else.

For weeks, my wife had been talking about getting him a rug for the room. We could have settled on a wash cloth. There was no place to put the big stuff and no reason to bring the little stuff.

"Honey, what's with the curtains?"

"So no one can see in."

"But he's on the third floor facing trees. Are you worried about peeping parrots?"

"And honey, why did you buy him a dish soap dispenser?"

"So he can wash his dishes."

I wondered.

Does a kid who hasn't washed a dish in 18 years, and is shipped off with enough paper goods and plastic utensils to fill a McDonald's rest stop, really need a kitchen caddy to organize his sponges, scrubbers and brushes?

I would have pressed the issue, but my hernia was kicking in from carrying

Our oldest graduates from SUNY Cobleskill in 2007.

boxes of food up three flights of stairs. If this kid fails in his studies, he can set up a bed and breakfast.

And he can't buy food here? You mean they don't have any supermarkets in central New York? Were Sullivan County's Ramen noodles that much better?

"Honey, so … why are we bringing up so much food?"

"In case he gets hungry."

"But isn't that why we're giving this college all our money?"

This kid's gonna learn how to eat like a king, while we educate ourselves on the use of Hamburger Helper in the basic food groups.

My wife asked, "But what if he gets hungry in his room?"

"Then he'll know how I'll feel for the next four years."

Finally, we squeezed everything into the room – and managed to squeeze ourselves out.

We waited on line for an hour to register his car. Waited on line two hours to register him. Met his roommate. Nice kid. I think we're going to be OK with our Lecter fears. He's a vegetarian. The only thing left to do was leave. Alone. Without our firstborn.

At that moment, I wondered … was this the right school, had we prepared him for what lies ahead, would things ever be the same?

He gave his mom a hug. He let me kiss his cheek.

"Honey, you think he'll be OK?"

"He's fine. He's ready. And besides, he'll be home next weekend."

My son, the college student, coming home. I hope he brings us some food.

August 28, 2003

Vacation time, come hell or high heels

Watching my wife pack for our upcoming vacation, it occurred to me that because of weight restrictions on the airplane, we'd have to make a tough decision about boarding.

The way I figured, there won't be room on the flight for both her shoes and me.

Not unless I squeeze my way into a couple of slingbacks, hide a few sandals in my sports coat and tuck her pumps in my pants — which might get me through security but would leave me in intense pain once the "fasten seat belt" light comes on.

While she'll see the ruins of ancient Rome in a pair of Roberto Cavallis, meander through Monte Carlo wearing Marc Ecko and gallivant in Greece in the soles of Giuseppa Zanotti, I'll be left behind to schlep around Sullivan in worn Chuck Taylors.

This seems only fitting, since I never considered "buying shoes" a critical element in planning for a cruise. Big mistake.

My wife has spent the past 18 months studying up on sandals, trying to figure out the trajectory of the hook and loop as compared with the ankle strap and asking the age-old question: Can a woman find happiness wearing an open toe while her round-toe, pointy-toe and moc-toe shoes sit idly by?

I, on the other hand, wondered if a clean pair of Converse, fully laced, could pass for formal dining on the cruise.

When I "suggested" to my wife that she might want to "consider" pruning her shoe tree down from a giant redwood to a manageable hedge, she quickly countered with a question that I could not answer:

"OK, and what would you suggest I wear with all these new outfits I bought for the trip?"

In my younger years, I might have suggested a clean pair of Converse, but my reflexes have slowed a bit, and I don't think I can duck as quickly as she can toss a loafer.

But I am concerned that she has turned our bedroom into a showroom that the folks at Macy's would be proud to call their own. And in no small part, they should — since until recently, all the clothes hanging in our bedroom had been hanging in their store.

I don't mean to exaggerate, but the other day some woman stopped me as I tried to carry the laundry basket into our room because I was bringing in too many items.

The only diversion from her marathon shopping spree was when she eyed my choice of accompanying attire, leaving her nearly speechless — except for the occasional, "You're not really planning to wear that?"

While my idea of fine, albeit well-broken-in outfits, seemed to go fine with those laced-up Cons, I thought it wise to take heed from her plea not to look like Captain Jack Sparrow preparing for a journey on the Black Pearl. I asked what colors she was bringing so we might match for the pictures.

She said she'd have to check her trip book.

Folks, the scientists working at mission control did less planning to put a man on the moon than my wife has in getting us ready to for this trip.

It's her alphabetized, color-coded and pocket-sized manual that puts Rand McNally to shame. No detail was left to chance, and no chance she left out any detail.

From what we need to buy to what we need to pack. From shore excursions to ship activities with a precise listing of where we go, when we go, how we get there and what we'll see. She just added a chapter on who to call for help and who to call if help comes late. If Amelia Earhart had anything close to my wife's travel book, she'd still be around telling us about her flight. And what she wore that day.

And in between the list of U.S. consulates and favorite foreign phrases was her months of planning, weeks of matching and days of final decision-making list of what she'll wear. For the days and nights, if hot or cold, indoors or out, by the pool or near the Pope.

The woman is ready. I am not. But we'll give it a go. If only I can find something to wear with red pumps.

August 30, 2007

Vacuuming at light speed

I had an easier time figuring out how to downshift in a car than I had trying to work our new Dyson vacuum cleaner.

Have you seen this thing?

Reminds me of a Star Wars espresso maker.

Even has a wand that looks like one of those dueling Jedi Lightsabers that you could use if a pesky dust bunny decides to hide over in the dark side of the corner.

This is not your mother's Hoover. I know this because I can run your mother's Hoover. And I've done pretty well running my wife's old beige Electrolux.

That's a simple machine. Plug it in, push the button at the top and VRR-ROOOMMM, it picks up the dirt.

Admittedly, not always on the first shot. But it's not like the machine isn't trying. It's older. Like a lot of us. Not everything works on the first try. So I didn't mind vacuuming over a spot a second time.

Then one day I find the Electrolux is gone. Relegated to the attic as a backup, its services no longer needed.

"You'll love the Dyson," said my wife, giddy as she showed off the purple stair tool, the purple brush tool, the purple flexi crevice tool and, finally, the purple Dyson.

"And here it is." she screams, shaking as this monstrosity is pulled from the box. "The DC 14 ... complete with the DC 14 wand!"

I wasn't sure if we had gotten a vacuum cleaner or an airplane.

"But what about the Electrolux?" I asked, as if finding out my best friend had moved. "It worked. And I knew how to use it."

"It'll be the backup."

"A backup?"

"Honey, this is a Dyson."

She said it with such reverence that I expected to hear angels sing as she uttered the name.

Dyson.

This is the machine invented by James Dyson, a British chap who got so frustrated with the suction in his old vacuum that he would spend the next 15 years of his life trying to invent a vacuum cleaner with better suction.

Fifteen years because of bad suction? You can get less time for felony assault.

I don't know if suction is a big deal with all the British or just Mr. Dyson.

You've seen the commercial. Thin guy with the Julius Caesar haircut who boasts about how he came up with more than 5,000 prototypes.

The man couldn't sleep because his vacuum bag was always getting clogged up.

One time he even ripped the bag out of the machine.

Maybe somebody should have taken the vacuum bag away from Dyson and got him a cup of decaffeinated tea.

In fact, Dyson spent 15 years making 5,127 prototypes, testing all different kinds of dust. If I only knew. I could have saved him at least a decade. Maybe longer.

One week in our boys' room and Dyson would have experienced a smorgasbord of shmutz. Dirt everywhere. Some of it even prehistoric.

The big deal with the Dyson is that you don't need a vacuum bag or a filter. All the dirt and dust end up in a place Dyson calls "the shroud."

Apparently, the machine separates dirt and dust from the airflow using centrifugal force. That's what he says.

Personally, I'm not about to waste a second – let alone 15 years – checking to see if the dirt and dust are separated. And how can you tell? When dust piles up, doesn't it become dirt? I know some dirt, without naming names, that can get pretty dusty.

Besides, I had more important things to figure out, like where they put the "on" switch for this vacuum of the future.

After 15 years, you'd figure the guy would have given a minute to making it easier to start the damn thing.

I released the hose. I let loose the DC 14 wand, took off the brush bar, loosened the upper cord hook from the lower cord and created a malfunction in the airway inspection valve. I believe I cut off power to Utica before I finally got it started.

And yes, it works.

With a simple press of the button, I was up the stairs with the purple Dyson still at the landing, the DC 14 hose allowing me to track dust bunnies lurking in a galaxy far, far away.

I feel your power, Obi-Wan Dyson.

May the suction force be with you.

August 18, 2005

Barry and Boo Boo and Friends

Times Herald-Record photo by Tom Bushey

Finest in funerals
for our furry friend

What do you say at the funeral service for a guinea pig, especially when the two of you weren't that close?

Nothing much.

So the boys and I dug some earth, buried and covered up Woody Lewis, allowing nature to take its course with our once faithful furry friend.

I call it the fast-food funeral.

In and out for less than a buck.

Sure, I had considered the options.

Maybe Woody would have wanted an afterlife similar to the guinea pigs of the rich and famous.

I went online to visit the Hartsdale Pet Cemetery and Cremator, which calls itself "America's First and Most Prestigious Pet Burial Grounds."

They encourage pet owners to consider the pre-need plots so that a pet may receive the kind of final tribute they wish.

Woody always kept things simple. Wasn't fussy about his lettuce or what constituted a bathroom. But it was too late to ask, so I kept an open mind and moved down the list of options.

They offered a wide variety of "reasonably" priced caskets and vaults of the most reputable brand names.

That wouldn't have worked for Woody. He never cared for brand items. It's what we liked about him.

They asked if I wanted a private room at the funeral where a few moments of peace and solitude could be spent. Maybe I'd want services by a religious figure.

We adopted Woody when he was just a few weeks old. I wasn't sure about his faith, but I was guessing the guinea pig wasn't Jewish. At this time, aren't we all God's children?

At Hartsdale, their commitment to plot holders is year-round.

Woody would be surrounded by chrysanthemums in the spring and begonias in summer. A special covering in early December would include colorfully decorated wreaths of balsam and spruce. Not bad for someone who usually settled for wood chips.

Of course they included no prices. Because if you have to ask ...

And really, should money be an object?

It's not like we didn't like Woody.

What was not to like?

He didn't leave underwear in the hallway, didn't smell up the bathroom and didn't wear his pants around his thighs.

Makes you wonder just where to place teen-agers on the old food chain.

Most of the time Woody would hang out around the cage, occasionally do a few laps on his wheel and gnaw on a salt lick stone.

At times he was so quiet we couldn't tell if he was sleeping or …

And that might have been his problem.

Try ignoring your dog. I know you wouldn't want to, but just try.

Especially when it tilts its head in that curious way and looks at you with those big brown puppy dog eyes.

It barks when it's time to eat, jumps at you for attention and nuzzles under your arm when you're trying to read the paper.

And if you really ignore the dog it poops on your rug.

Hard not to notice.

We had no such problems from Woody, who always went for the simple things in life.

Hartsdale was no place for Woody.

It's not like we just dumped him in the woods.

Or had him meet his maker in the porcelain tunnel of tomorrow – a final journey with the Tidy Bowl man.

No, we wanted Woody's final resting place to be near the house. Even picked out a brand new shoe box, complete with the special tissues that come with the shoes.

The boys suggested the shaded spot near the old oak tree.

Have you ever tried to dig under an old oak tree? You'd have better luck blasting under the tree.

After 20 minutes of attempted digging I wasn't sure who was going to wind up in the hole.

We compromised. Woody would go in the hole, but the shoe box would remain topside.

Then we encircled some rocks around Woody, placed three sticks to mark his plot and headed inside.

I'll miss Woody Lewis, although I can't tell you why. Maybe it's because he didn't ask much from us, and got even less in return. Or that we just knew he was there, making noise on his wheel or from the salt lick stone.

He was a good guinea pig. As guinea pigs go.

March 28, 2002

Dustin out with Ginger.

A lot of friend
in a five-pound ball of fluff

I was never a fan of small dogs.

For one thing, they're small. Wimpy and small. Noisy and small. Like they have to yap to compensate for their size. The less dog there is, the louder they have to be. Napoleon was like that.

Toss a Frisbee at one of these toy dogs and you'll give them a concussion.

All of which is why I didn't immediately warm up to the moving surprise my wife had cuddled in her arms – the latest mouth to feed in the Lewis house, a white Pomeranian the kids would name Ginger.

"It's a cuuute dog," my wife suggested.

"It's a fur ball with teeth."

"You'll learn to like her."

"I better learn to watch where I walk – or I'll accidentally squish the little fur ball with teeth."

This was a toy dog that could be a toy for toy dogs.

I made my intentions clear.

It would be my wife's dog. The boys' dog. If the goldfish wanted to bat her around for a while, that was fine by me.

I'd watch her from afar.

Then a funny thing happened.

Their pet became my problem.

Ginger needed to be fed. Needed to go out and needed a bath.

Unlike the boys, who long ago escaped the confines of the kitchen sink, Ginger, at about two feet in length, was just the right size for the extra-deep porcelain spa, complete with spray nozzle.

You want to know what a five-pound Pomeranian looks like soaking wet? A two-pound rat. But it was my drowned rat, who I begrudgingly admitted wasn't that bad a dog.

She really didn't yap that much. She could handle herself wrestling around the house, and her favorite toy was a rubber newspaper, the "Daily Growl."

When I went to pick up my son from play practice, he asked that I bring Ginger. How sweet. He missed the dog.

As I got to the school he cradled the dog in his arms.

"Babe magnet," he whispered.

Sure enough, within seconds he was surrounded by the girls in his class, who couldn't get over the cute white fur ball with the sleepy brown eyes. When Ginger wasn't being used as a pawn to advance my son's love life, she slouched along the top of the couch, positioned under the front picture window.

This penthouse view allowed her to bathe under the warmth of the midday sun. She would emerge from her beauty nap and stretch to look out just as the school bus slowed to the driveway.

Then on cue, Ginger would go from doggie diva to faithful fido, ready to welcome her conquering brothers from … well, wherever she thought that noisy yellow bus takes them.

At night, she would get comfortable on our laps. Our "West Wing" companion.

For the last couple of years, Ginger has been my walking mate, my personal alarm clock who made sure a little thing like sleep on the weekend wouldn't stand in the way of our early morning trek.

Together we braved the elements.

I'd take a step. She'd take six. Going up the hill she was by my side. On the way down she'd get even and want to gallop. She was my spunky Pomeranian.

She'd look around, making sure there weren't any killer squirrels or nasty earthworms to get in our way. After scaring off one cat, she give me a glance, making sure I knew she had my back.

Our last walk was cut short. Ginger wasn't able to keep up. She tried. But the legs weren't moving. She settled for the carpet instead of her penthouse view on the couch.

Wasn't in the mood to wrestle.

When my kids and wife were out of the house Sunday, I packed up the hair brush that helped turn my wet rat into a puffy Pomeranian. I put away her "Daily Growl" toy.

We had buried her the day before, not far from where the noisy yellow bus drops off the boys and where I begin my morning walk.

I walked my usual walk Monday morning. But I didn't have my small dog to scare away the squirrels and earthworms.

July 17, 2003

I wish Boo Boo would stop reading over my shoulder.

The ritual drama
of my Boo Boo making poo poo

There are few things that humble me more than when I'm forced to slowly trudge around and around and around in a foot of snow, the temperature hovering near zero, the wind smacking me in the face, as I wait for my Boo Boo to find just the right spot to poop.

Can one small drift really make a difference?

Makes you wonder who is getting walked.

I suppose the only thing more humbling would be having to pick up that poop, but the way I figure, what's the point of taking out a second mortgage and paying taxes if you can't leave your dog's poop on the lawn?

I can be pretty picky when it comes to getting the right pair of shoes or ordering off the menu. I'll drive for miles on empty searching for cheap gas. But when I'm at the stadium and the urge hits, anything open will do just fine. And from the size of the line, no one is being too particular.

I'm not really sure Boo Boo even needs to circle around as much as she does. Going strictly on observation, I'd bet money she does far less circling in the warm weather months. I think that all this circling around in the snow is just a way to punish me for not devising some sort of indoor plumbing for her.

"Boy, it's cold out here. Sniff. Sniff. Glad I've got all this fur. Suppose I could poop right now and then we can both go inside. Sniff. Sniff. Naaaaahhh. I think he's shivering. Good. I'll circle some more. Sniff. Sniff."

I think she smirks with every sniff. Call it payback.

Not that I blame her.

Our options might be limited, but who among us would love having to squat in the snow.

I give her credit for putting up with this system.

We might treat her like she's one of the family, but to the best of my knowledge, she's the only one living under our roof who must go outside to urinate. Even the boys will draw the line when it comes to relieving themselves.

I'm sure there are dog trainers who can't believe what they're reading.

I can hear them screaming about how I let this get out of hand, how vital it is to have a properly potty-trained dog and how important it is for an animal to go on command from its owner:

"Now drop and give me number two!"

I don't know.

It just can't be that pleasant, forced to go out in the open, in front of other dogs, not to mention those cats and squirrels. You just know they're getting a kick watching Mr. Tough Bark be told where and when to go.

And that comes after she goes through the indignity of having to wait and whimper by the door for someone to take her out.

"Guys, Boo Boo has to go out!"

"I walked her yesterday, it's Daniel's turn!"

"I walked her this afternoon, it's Dustin's turn!"

"But I fed her yesterday, so Daniel has to walk her!"

"I checked her water, Dustin walks her now!"

By this point Boo Boo is sweating up a storm and hopping around as if she was trying to avoid hot coals.

Eventually someone (yours truly) takes pity on our Pomeranian.

When Boo Boo finally stops spinning and gets down to business, I like to turn my head.

Give her a little privacy.

The least I could offer her is some scintilla of self-respect. Take away the pressure of the moment.

And when she's done:

"Goooooooood giiiiiiirrrl."

She wags her tail. All is forgiven.

Until the next time she scratches at the door.

January 12, 2006

Barry's Life as a Dad

Taking Bonnie to my high school prom at Kutsher's in 1978. She's smiling because I've pinned my finger to her chest.

Tell the man you want a fluffy blue shirt

'D'ustin, are you gonna ask them if they have the blue shirt?"

"Dad, I'm not getting a puffy blue shirt."

"It's not puffy. Seinfeld called it 'puffy.' It's a fluffy blue shirt. It has ruffles that makes it fluffy – not puffy."

"Dad, no one wears those anymore. Here, look in the book. Do you see any of the guys wearing a puffy blue shirt?"

"That's fluffy. What about your brother? He'll wear the fluffy blue shirt."

"Daniel, are you going to ask about the blue shirt?"

"The one with things in the front?"

"The ruffles. Yeah!"

"No."

"Why?"

"It'll look stupid."

"You walk around with your pants half-way down your underwear – and you think a fluffy blue shirt looks stupid."

"I won't like it."

"You've never seen it."

"You're wearing it in your prom picture?"

"Yeah, that's it. Doesn't it look good?"

Left: Three amigos at World Disney World.

"It looks stupid."

"Do me a favor. When the man asks what kind of shirt you want, tell him you want to try on the fluffy blue shirt. It'll look good with the white tux."

"Dad, we're both getting a black tux."

"You're not getting white?"

"Black!"

"And no fluffy blue shirts? Fine. Anyway, I'll have the car looking good when I take you and your dates to the prom. You can even play your music on the drive."

"Dad, you don't have to drive us, we rented a limo."

"You rented a limo? You don't have jobs, how can you rent a limo?"

"We work weekends."

"You've worked weekends for three months. I've worked weekdays for 23 years and I've never rented a limo. I don't even know how much it costs."

"It'll cost about five hundred dollars – but we get it for seven hours."

"But you'll be at the prom all night?"

"Yeah, but we had to rent it for the whole night. Don't worry, two other couples are going. It's a good deal. Besides, now you won't have to drive us to the place. You said it was an hour one way."

"That's another thing. Your class couldn't find anyplace in Sullivan County to have a prom? We have nice restaurants here. And a few hotels. You know, I took your mom to my prom at Kutsher's."

"You've told us, Dad."

"What, your class is too good for Kutsher's? Your mom had her prom in the school gym. There are kids who still have proms in the gym. Kutsher's is 20 minutes from here. Then you wouldn't have needed the limo."

"By the way Dad, we have to buy prom tickets. It's a hundred dollars."

"A hundred bucks?"

"Yeah, Dad, but that's not for one person. It's a hundred dollars for a couple."

"A hundred bucks to get into the prom and five hundred to get to the prom?"

"It's actually more like six hundred."

"Six hundred?"

"Yeah, we have to tip the driver."

"I've been driving you guys around for 16 years and I never saw a tip. Your limo is going to cost more than I paid for my first car, which I used for my own prom. And I had that car a lot longer than seven hours."

"You're talking about your Gremlin?"

"Yeah. It was a great car."

"You said it was a lemon."

"Later, but for the first couple of weeks that I had it on the road, it was great. And the night of the prom, I threw a blanket in the back so you couldn't see the cinder blocks. Maybe I can rent you a Gremlin."

"Dad, what do you think of this black jacket? I'm gonna pick out a white shirt … Daniel's going to wear a black shirt. And we asked the guy … he says they don't sell blue ruffled shirts."

"It's OK. Stand still. Let me look at both of you. You're right, the black tux looks nice. Makes you guys look taller. Older. Looks nice. Let's go tell your mom."

May 05, 2005

Good friends; Dustin, Devin Kaminski, Daniel and Scott Squires before the limo arrives.

"Dad, do we have to listen to your music when we drive?

Dread on the parallel path
to freedom

They are the words that can turn any cocky teenager into a quivering jelly-fish. Words that can spell doom, signal confinement and delay the freedom last experienced when the training wheels came off the bicycle.

Will it be heard after the street light?

Halfway down the side street?

Or maybe in the middle of Broadway in Monticello during the midday rush when you can't imagine anyone being crazy enough to ask a 16-year-old, especially one who doesn't even have a driver's license, to attempt squeezing a midsize car into a space hardly big enough for a scooter.

Oh, teens can pray all they want that between the request for the three-point-turn, making sure all stops are complete stops and being aware that pedestrians (even slooowww moving pedestrians) have the right-of-way, that possibly the person with the clipboard will forget the command.

They wish.

Just as sure as pimples will bloom on the eve of the prom – you can bet those words will be said with the determination of a drill sergeant giving orders to a new recruit:

"OK … now I want you to parallel park."

Isn't it amazing how one simple sentence can bring a tear to the eye of an otherwise fearless teen – yet at the same time make a parent sigh with relief?

The parallel park.

It's what separates the car driver from the vehicle operator.

Sure, Dale Earnhardt Jr. can drive a car 190 mph and just keep turning left for three hours. But can he shoehorn that No. 8 between a pair of minivans with a 2-foot snow-bank on the curb and traffic coming up on his rear?

On the first try?

For parents, it's our momentary reprieve from what we reluctantly admit is the inevitable.

Do we really want our kids to drive?

What are ya, crazy?

Do we want them to be free, to travel the world and not be tied down to us old folks at home? Yeah.

But I say wait till us old folks are dead.

Just the thought of giving my teens the keys is going to put me in an early grave. I've tried my best to keep our twin moths from becoming monarchs.

Much to their chagrin.

"Daaad, don't worry, we know how to drive. Schedule the road test."

"I will."

"When?"

"You need more practice. Besides, you don't want to take a road test in the summer. There are people walking all over the place in the summer. You think they'll give you a license if you hit someone?"

That was last summer.

We practiced some more in the fall. I told them they shouldn't take their road test with all the leaves falling. The colors could be a real distraction for a new driver.

Then came winter and I told them nobody wants to take a road test on slushy roads. Besides, I said, you need to practice on snow.

That lasted me through mid-February.

The only thing more tiring than the snow is my excuses for delaying a road test. I know they know how to drive. But I know it's not enough to pass the test.

Not until they can: PARALLEL PARK.

It's an art.

And not every attempt is a masterpiece.

I know veterans of the road who find a spot and start out strong.

Signal. Move up to the car just ahead. Slowly inch back, cutting when your front wheel is along side the rear bumper of the front car. Move back. Cut. Back. Cut.

Next thing you know your rear tire is hitting the curb and most of the front is sticking out like a piñata waiting to be hit.

You move up, back up and hit the car behind you. Move up and hit the car in front.

After 10 minutes of playing bumper cars you're in the spot. Unfortunately, it's two feet from the curb.

My boys say they're ready. I think they are. We'll find out today.

Remember, two hands on the wheel. Keep looking in the mirror. Don't forget to signal. Watch out for pedestrians.

If not this time, next time. Or the time after that.

They'll get their freedom. It's inevitable.

March 03, 2005

Parents know cookie dough is a tough sell

'Say, Bob, how about some cookie dough?"

"Cookie dough?"

"Sure, cookie dough. How about a three-pound pail of sugar cookie dough?"

"Gee, Barry, that sounds like an awful lot of cookie dough."

"Bob, can you really have too much cookie dough? I mean, you've got the holidays coming up, weekends by the fire. Halloween."

"Yeah, but …"

"Right, it's the perfect treat for those little ghouls and goblins. And what better way to give them the pep to go house after house after house than a handful of some fresh homemade sugar cookies, straight from your own three-pound supply of cookie dough?"

"Barry, are you selling this stuff?"

"Not for me. For my son. And I'm not really selling. More like helping out the high school band. You know, instruments, music. It's the cost of sending your kids to school."

"But, Barry, didn't they just raise your taxes to cover that higher cost of sending your kids to school?"

"You know, Bob, that's what I thought. But I guess it's not enough. Especially since they keep building. New auditorium. New cafeteria. New classrooms."

"But, Barry, wasn't there a separate building project to pay for that construction?"

"Bob, what's a parent to do? So, how about those cookies?"

"That's a lot of sugar, Barry, isn't it?"

"Right you are, Bob. What was I thinking? For the same price, I'll order you three pounds of healthy oatmeal raisin cookie dough. You'll be the envy of the block."

"But three pounds?"

"Let me tell ya, this stuff will last you till spring. Not crazy about raisins? How about chocolate chunk cookie dough. It's only 50 cents more, but, hey Bob, chocolate chunks. How many three pound tubs can I put you down for? Don't even need the money now."

"Barry, we're trying to watch our weight, and besides, I don't know if cookies are the best Halloween treat. You know, giving out unwrapped food."

"Right you are, Bob. What was I thinking? Forget the cookies. How about socks?"

"You're selling socks?"

"Not for me, Bob. It's for my son. His Future Business Leaders of America club. So, Bob, are you a low cut kind-of-guy or strictly ¼-crew."

"Barry, I've got plenty of socks."

"Not like these, Bob. They have little American flags. How about your initials?"

"Barry, do the socks pay for club trips?"

"No, Bob, I still got to pay for the trips. Gotta pay for everything. I'm not really sure why he's selling socks. But at least it's better than selling cheese."

"Cheese?"

"Sharp cheddar? Almond Cheese Log? For $7.50 I can get you a whole Garden Herb Snack spread."

"Let me guess, Barry, another school club?"

"Right you are, Bob. The more organizations my kids belong to, the more I get to sell. Let's see, yearbook's got cheesecake, future farmers are doing flower bulbs, Spanish club has wrapping paper and I thought I heard something about the football team and scented candles. You know, Bob, it's hard to keep up."

"Barry, why don't you have your kids sell the stuff."

"Would love to, Bob, but they don't have the time. Between school and all these different clubs, they barely squeeze out a moment for homework."

"Have them quit the clubs."

"Would love to, Bob, but you can't get into college unless you're diversified."

"So tell me, Barry, how are you gonna pay for college?"

"Bob, how about six months of gourmet nuts?"

October 02, 2003

Get a little closer Dustin so I can see your mustache.

The folly-cle
of a teenager's first mustache

To shave or not to shave.

That was the question.

Even after he emptied a can of shaving cream on his face, covering every nook and cranny of every present and potential facial follicle, our son still wasn't sure if he was ready to celebrate his 16th birthday by removing his mustache.

That's what he called it.

His mustache.

Tom Selleck had a mustache. Albert Einstein had a mustache. Gene Shalit has a mustache.

What our teen has is a shadow above his lip.

I wondered if not seeing his mustache shadow meant we'd have six more weeks of spring?

But be it real or imaginary, the burden of his facial hair was weighing heavy on his mind – and putting an unusual strain on my senses.

"Can you feel this ... right here, you feel this ... it's rough, isn't it?" he'd routinely ask, pushing his cheek into my face, making sure I, too, got to experience his adolescent growth.

"Feels like sandpaper, doesn't it?"

I told him I could certainly feel the paper part, but I was having some trouble with the grains of sand.

OK. But I certainly couldn't miss the mustache?

"Look, right here ... you see this, here ... no, not there ... here ... right over here," moving in to give me an up close and personal look up his nostril – where there was an abundance of hair.

I thought if he pushed his nose up any more, the thing would fall right off.

"Should I shave it or just trim it?"

I was hoping he was talking about his nose hairs, but clearly he was seeking grooming tips about his shadow, uh, mustache.

So before he attempted to cut a single hair or shed a drop of blood – my fear is that he'd lose more blood than hair – I figured it was time to issue him the warning.

Yes, the warning.

Also known as the other father and son talk.

Ever since the first teen tried to scrape a really sharp rock over his face, dads have issued the warning:

"Son, once you shave with that adjustable double-edged rock, you'll be scraping your face with a rock for the rest of your life."

"The hair will return day after day, coming in thicker and thicker. Go a day without shaving, and you'll look like a woolly mammoth."

Following the wisdom of my ancestors, I looked at my son through the bathroom mirror, the bottom half of his face all white with lather. He looked more like Santa minus the red suit than my youngest ready to grow up before my eyes.

"It'll grow in thicker?"

"Thicker."

"Every day?"

"I know some guys who get a 5 o'clock shadow by lunch."

With that, he rinsed the razor under the hot water. With the steady hand of a surgeon, he carefully lifted his right hand to his upper lip. With the left hand, he moved his nose to the side.

It was a clean stroke.

"Is it gone?" he asked, as if he had lost an old friend.

"Well, the lather is gone, but the shadow's still there."

I suggested the hair might come off more quickly if he took the safety cover off the razor.

A second later, his shadow was gone.

He touched up cheeks and chin and bathed in some after-shave.

"Too much?"

"I usually keep it to less than half a bottle, but you want to be sure the first time."

He eyed the mirror, inspecting his work. "Guess I'm getting old, huh?"

I looked back in the mirror, admiring my early Father's Day gift. A tie is nice.

Teaching your son to shave – priceless.

June 17, 2004

Teeth remind of special time

I still have the tooth. In fact, I have all of them ... every incisor, bicuspid and molar. The ones that were accidentally freed when the wrestling match in the living room got out of hand and the ones purposely loosened by a jack-hammer-like tongue when the need for cash took precedent over a gap-toothed smile.

I didn't make a conscientious effort to keep them ... I just never thought about throwing them out. I still have my junior high bus pass. Why would I throw out my kids' teeth?

Unlike my baseball card collection, I don't have any desire to scatter them across the floor and study the details. Or wonder how much the ones in mint condition are worth. It's not like I stay up late and play forensic odontologist, trying to figure out if I can match the bicuspid with the boy.

As gory as keeping them might be, I just couldn't toss them in the trash or watch them be flushed away.

So, for more then a decade, I've filled several old film canisters that only saw the light of day when the tooth fairy magically turned the molar into money. I can't remember the going rate in the early '90s, but these days don't even bother making the switch unless you'll willing to fork over a greenback.

If I had given it any thought, I would have collected their dirty socks and under-wear, piled in the corner of their room, a monument to the God of nasty.

Even the dog, that'll sniff just about anything, backs away from that pile.

Maybe I should have kept their collection of three-wheel Match Box cars, head-less action figures and the Trouble game that was down two blues pieces within seconds of it being opened.

I could have held on to the lumps of Play-Dough, which lost some of its elastic-ity after being left uncovered since '92.

That all got thrown out. But I kept the teeth.

Like the rings that surround a tree trunk, the teeth in some odd way have marked the passage of time, for both myself and the boys. Along with a trip down memory lane in a never-ending battle to fight tooth decay, my cherished pieces of enamel are constant reminders of their youth, when life was as simple as finding buried treasure under a pillow.

(Up the music to Sunrise, Sunset).

These days, I'm ready to stick my head under the pillow as I come to grips with having three teen-age boys in our house.

Without warning, I've suddenly become old. And without provocation, I've been warned over and over how I "just don't get it."

Not that I ever wanted it, or had the urge to need it. And maybe I am old, because I don't even remember talking about it. All I know is not to count on it, because the boys keep reminding me that I'm not getting it.

Since I'm deteriorating before their eyes, I thought it would be wise to have these strong young men with their keen senses help their fossilized folks.

But, alas, the aging process seems to be inherent, because they've already forgotten that dirty dishes become clean when placed IN the dishwasher - not at the foot of their beds.

I must remind them that the school bus does not make trips up our stairs. In order to make it to class, they must get OUT of bed.

And despite the advances in home technology, our toilets do not flush on their own. Our teens need to do their part.

But I'm sure the boys will eventually get the hang of all this, especially now that they are all teens, on the threshold of making their way in the world.

Meanwhile the dad that "doesn't get it" will hold on to his film canisters full of teeth, remembering when the boys weren't planning their future, but how they would spend their tooth fairy money.

May 31, 2001

Last partings
are such sweet sorrow

As we near the home stretch in this year of "lasts" for our high school seniors, few of the must-have-tissues events have provided as many mixed emotions as our son's last high school band concert.

There were the usual tears of joy from this milestone moment, as the lads in their pressed white shirts and the girls in their pretty black dresses filled the old gymnasium with the sounds that would make every mom and dad proud.

There were the predictable tears of sorrow, knowing that we may have been witnessing our child's last musical performance, a journey that began more than a decade ago when he wet his whistle trying to master "Hot Cross Buns." Now he was settling in to play Mozart's "Concert Rondo."

But mostly we shed tears of pain from having to sit for more than two hours on those tush-numbing metal chairs that school districts buy in bulk from the U.S. government, which pulled them out of the Guantanamo Bay camps because of the cruel and unusual punishment they inflicted on prisoners.

And folks wonder if these school concerts leave a lasting impression on friends and relatives.

I say that we "witnessed" our son's last concert with a touch of blind faith, since we didn't actually see him perform.

Truth be known - we've never really "seen" him perform. It's the curse of the baritone player.

Every year, every concert, they seat him in the back row, off to the right. And we begin the evening with this familiar overture:

"Do you see him?"

"I don't see him. Do you see him?"

"I don't think I see him?"

"Wait is that him with the sticks?"

"That's a redhead who plays the drums. Our kid is a blond who plays the baritone."

"Yeah, but at least I can see that kid."

Two years ago, our son was positioned just right of the alto saxophone and a hair to the left of the trombone, so if we slouched just a smidgen, tilted our heads about 45 degrees and squinted so that we could barely see the stage, we were able to make out the tapping of his shoes. That's as close as we got.

Next year, take a clue from volleyball and just rotate the band. Play a note and everyone moves to the next chair. Next note, next chair. There may be time for only one song, but everyone gets a chance to sit in the front.

Our son has played since fourth grade. That's about two concerts a year, which I figure equals no less than 35 hours of squirming in those metal chairs. And the only part of our son we ever caught was his tapping black shoes.

Still, we never missed a beat. You go to the games whether your child plays or not, and you go to the school plays no matter what your child's part is. We never even gave a second thought to missing a concert.

That's not exactly true. There were many nights when the last thing I wanted to do was sit in a 50-year-old gym, no air in the summer, no heat in the winter, and wait.

We knew to wait until the end, just like we knew we'd never seen our son perform. The band's always last.

So we'd listen to the junior high and the high school chorus, the women's and the men's chorus, the jazz band and student ensemble. In some years, the students would perform solos and teachers would sing.

Concerts took so long they'd promote the kids at intermission.

Last week, the curtain rose on the last concert. True to form, the band was last, and our son was in the back, off to the right.

The four songs went fast. Faster than I remember.

Just like that, the curtain came down.

I looked over the program. It seemed short.

Said bye to a few parents - same group that I see at every concert - not sure that I'll see these folks again. Thanked the principal for taking pictures of the kids.

The music teacher came by, asked if we heard our son's solo.

"Loud and clear."

The old gym was nearly empty when our son arrived, baritone in hand.

"Did you see me?"

"Yeah, you're in the back. Just to the right. And I heard that solo. Sounded real nice."

Funny, most years, I couldn't wait to get out of that metal seat. This time I just sat for a while.

June 15, 2006

Notice the artwork in Sean's dorm.

Barry's Tips
For Your Child's Dorm

As we prepared to send our oldest child off for yet another year of college, I couldn't help but notice his unique packing style.

Very retro.

It dated all the way back to May, when he emptied his dorm room onto a corner of our garage floor.

Bed sheets. Blankets. Rugs. Clothes.

It left me wondering.

Was summer really over? Was our son really leaving already? And was he really about to put his dirty pile of laundry that had been sitting in our garage for three months into my clean car?

Amazing. Three months and the pile hadn't moved an inch. Not by human hands, at least.

I'm guessing some four-, eight- and sixteen-legged creatures had moved into the pile, which was beginning to give off some unusual fumes.

My wife said I was making a mountain out of a mole hill. OK, but was it troubling her that our son was making a compost pile out of his bed linen?

To be honest, folks, I wasn't sure if I should share that story with you – airing our son's dirty laundry, pun intended, in public.

But then I thought, you're not going to find the saga of the summer-old college laundry in any of those "Tips For Your Child's Dorm" articles that newspapers and magazines run this time of year.

Sure, they'll share with you secrets on how to make the most of your child's closet, how throw pillows will brighten the room and how to limit the clutter.

One "tip" I read said to buy 100 percent Egyptian cotton sheets for your college student – to show you care.

Do these people have children?

Another suggested ways that our son could maximize the flow of positive chi in his dorm room and increase the essence of space.

Here's my suggestion to increase the flow of feng shui in his dorm room. He might want to start with picking up his underwear and taking down the decorative police crime-scene tape.

If it's not too late, let me offer you a few of my own tips that should save everyone a lot of time and money. And isn't that the least we should get out of our child's college education?

- Chances are that your child has not given a second thought to cleaning any of the cups, plates and utensils that needed to be washed when brought home three months ago. Look close and you'll notice what looks like blue cotton stuffed into the cups. It's not blue cotton. And don't even look at the forks. Toss them. Right now.

- You'll need to get your child all new shower supplies. Soap holder. Towels. Nothing made it back home. Be very glad of that.

- You'll need to get new light bulbs to replace the ones that have paint and wax melted on them. Don't ask.

- Buy pens and paper. It didn't make your child's "must get" list. Don't worry about surge protectors and extension chords. They made the "must get" list.

- As you might have guessed, you don't have to worry about picking up dish soap. There's probably an unopened container in a box right next to the closed package of sponges, a half-dozen unused plug-in air fresheners and the never-touched dust pan and brush set that you bought last fall.

- You also won't need to buy laundry soap. Last year's box went unused. But you knew that already, given the amount of loads you washed during the school year.

- You'll need to get another set of those extra-long, extra-expensive, hard-to-find bed sheets. Apparently colleges provide beds – they're really nothing more than glorified army cots – that need special twin sheets. Go figure.

- But on the flip side, a single bed sheet will last the year. I know, you're asking how about getting a second sheet to put on while the first one is being washed. Trust me, the only time that sheet will get washed will be at Christmas, assuming it's not left in the dorm.

- Given what I just told you, why are worrying about the color of the duvet? Save your money and get extra napkins. Any color will do.

- Finally, make sure none of the laundry piles is moving before you pack them in the car.

August 25, 2005

School's open house
tests mind and lungs

I made my way down the hall, past the picture of last year's king and queen of the prom, past the poster about school ring deadlines and past the reminder that cookie dough orders are on their way.

I gave each one a passing glance.

There was no time to waste.

No time for idle chitchat with neighbors and friends.

No casual stroll down the hallway to check out the honor roll plaques.

You've got to stay focused when your school has Open House night. I know this, because I've been going to Open House night for more than a dozen years.

Parents visit their kid's school. Visit all their kid's teachers. Even sit where their kid sits.

But after two minutes of hearing my kids' teachers talk about tests and reports, projects and homework, I understand why my kids seem a bit overwhelmed – and very tired.

School is exhausting. And that's just getting to class.

At the start of Open House, the assistant principal gives us marching orders: Follow your kid's schedule.

Every parent has three minutes to get to their child's class and seven minutes to meet with the teacher. You can talk with the teacher, but don't conference with the teacher. You can sign up for a teacher conference and tell the teacher you're signing up for a conference, but don't talk to the teacher about the conference.

Remember seven minutes in the class … three minutes to get to class. While the assistant principal talked, I prepped.

My wife was working, so I was flying solo. No sweat. I had it all mapped out with the twins' schedules and a floor plan of the school. Sixteen classes in 90 minutes.

I'll pass on visiting the lunchroom staff.

The first bell rang and I was off – in search of Room 124: math.

This would be easy. Get to the classroom before the other parents, talk a little with one teacher and quickly head off to the other first-period teacher.

How hard could it be to find Room 124?

It's a small school.

I folded up the map and picked up my pace.

Room 136 … 134 … Piece of cake. Room 132 …

Most of the parents had found their classrooms. A few stragglers double-checked the map, but I was secure in the knowledge that 124 was just beyond the AV room and the library.

I glanced to my left … 113 … 112 …

I backpedaled … 112 … 113?

How do you get from 132 to 113?

The hall was now empty. I must have passed it.

Room 132 … 134 … 136 … cookie dough orders, class rings, nice picture of the king and queen. I pulled out the map. Room 124 was across from Room 109.

And they want to know why our kids can't pass math.

When I finally got to Room 124, I heard the teacher lecture the other parents on tardiness.

She stopped in midsentence.

"You're late, Mr. Lewis!"

I told her I'd love to stay after class, but I was late for English. And another math class. And soon, another English class.

By fourth period, I had lost my map and 10 pounds.

Kids don't need gym – they need oxygen.

I was getting dehydrated, so I signed up for the PTA so I could get a cookie and a cup of juice.

Rooms and teachers became a blur.

One teacher said she tests to the Regents. Another just worries about the Regents test.

I managed to ask one teacher how she comes up with a final grade. She said she takes the dozen or so quiz grades, multiplies it by three test grades and adds up the extra credit from unassigned homework to come up with a composite overall average.

I signed my wife up for the PTA to get another cookie and juice.

History repeated itself when I wound up going to one son's government class twice – but at the same time I forgot the other's parenting class.

I felt like I was failing parenting class.

The only class I made in three minutes was French.

The teacher was real nice. Was sympathetic to the long night I was having.

Said she gives homework, a couple of tests. But the class isn't about grades. It's learning a special language. Isn't that nice?

I even set up a conference for Tuesday. I only wish the boys actually took French.

September 30, 2004

Sometimes, wisdom means just being happy

OK, I'll give it a shot:
  Make sure you say please and thank you.
  Girls are attracted to bad boys, but they'll marry the good ones.
First thing people look at are your shoes.

No one likes a sore loser.

Wear clean underwear.

Share.

Listen.

It's all right to laugh.

If you go to the city, put a quarter in your shoe, so if you get mugged you'll be able to call for help.

Don't be stubborn. Ask for directions.

Enjoy what you do.

Those are the biggies.

I know there should be some pearls of wisdom or a quote from some Greek philosopher. Perhaps a biblical passage I could jot down that you can just pull out during troubled times.

Like Kipling traveling two roads.

Or a quip from Groucho Marx.

What would Ward tell Wally?

Seems like the time to offer up advice, but when I think of your future, I keep getting stuck in our past.

I can't remember … when was it when you didn't like your hair long; when it didn't matter if the Mets won or that you'd rather listen to Alan Jackson instead of Michael Jackson.

You now tower over your grandma, you're taller than your mother and when we talk it's eye-to-eye.

Not that we do an awful lot of talking.

No extended conversations, very little chit-chat about the weather. You grunt something about money, a cowboy hat and my music; I grunt back about going to work, wearing it in public and going deaf.

I ask, "Why do you have to play that stuff so loud?" and you come right back with, "What? You mean you didn't play your music loud? When the Beatles come on you blast us out. But what, I can't listen to what I like?"

Obviously, you listen better than I do.

And you're better at fixing a car. Have been for a while.

If it sputters, I look at the gas gauge and check the oil. You check the points and plugs. You can take out the whatchamacallit, replace it with a whosawhatza, and if need be, get a brand new whatchamacallit. I wish I could do that.

But I did teach you to drive. How to parallel park. Was it really just two years ago?

That was about the time you were filling the freezer with squirrel. I told you I'd cook it if you caught it, but I never thought you'd catch it.

Just like I thought you'd never last the ski season. Or track. You never quit. Never. Last place is a discouraging place, but you always found solace in reaching a personal best.

To be the best Boy Scout and hike the roughest terrain that New Mexico has to offer.

To be the best volunteer on the ambulance squad and use whatever down time you had to become a certified first responder. You passed the test on your first try.

I couldn't do that.

Just like I couldn't stand up and sing before hundreds of my peers at the state Future Farmers of America convention. But you did. You had courage. You had fun.

It's only now, when I see you in cap and gown, that I can appreciate the individual you've become. How proud I am of that individual.

And so I'll keep my advice simple.

Don't change.

June 26, 2003

Barry's Bucolic Life at Home

A running drip provides a chance to reinvent wheel

My wife woke me up in the middle of the night to ask if I could hear the running drip.

I told her I usually don't hear things when I'm sound asleep. But now that I was suddenly wide awake – yes, I could hear the running drip.

"Don't you want to know where it's coming from?"

Until a few moments earlier, I hadn't even cared that it existed. But my wife was happy to fill in the details.

"It's coming from the upstairs bathroom."

Clearly this was something she needed to share.

"Who's in the bathroom?"

"Not who. What. The running drip. Don't you hear the toilet running?"

Asleep in the middle of the night, I couldn't hear the running of the bulls, let alone the running drip in the toilet.

"Are you going to fix it?"

"Why, do you have to go to the bathroom?"

"We can't leave this. We're wasting water. It'll run the well dry. You've got to fix this."

I said fine, got up, went upstairs, jiggled the handle and went back to sleep.

The sound stopped so I figured I was in the clear.

You see, guys really don't care if the toilet runs.

I'm guessing most women are not surprised to hear about our disregard for the drip in the tank, given our propensity since childhood for the surprises we leave on the toilet seat.

But don't think apathy over a running toilet would ever keep us from proving once again how man can reinvent the wheel.

How else can we use our shiny, expensive tools?

My wife, upon further inspection, suggested replacing the seal on the fill valve.

Cost a few bucks. Take maybe an hour.

I could have done that.

Once I learned which piece was the fill valve.

Maybe some of you would have just replaced the seal. And knowing what I know today, that's what I should have done.

But nobody just replaces a seal on the "Do It Yourself" cable network. Not when there's an opportunity to replace the seal, the fill valve, the flapper, the

Left: Auditioning for Twisted Sister.

washers, some wing nuts, a gasket, the flush valve and anything else I could find in the tank.

So after three consecutive weekends of trying to disassemble the innards of our upstairs toilet, making numerous trips to the hardware store and buying enough tools so that someday I could open my own hardware store, I was ready to buy and build a new toilet tank.

Have you ever tried to build a new toilet tank?

Did you ever try to buy the pieces needed to build the tank?

Do you know how many different toilet repair kits you can buy?

"What's the tank you're replacing?" asked the awfully young looking clerk in my three time-zone long plumbing and hardware store.

"We've got Fluidmaster, American Standard, Kohler, Wellworth … you do know what you took out, right?"

I told him it was the kind where I jiggled the handle to make the drip stop.

Not the answer he was expecting.

"Well … do you want to replace it with the side or front handle? An adjustable flush flapper? And would you like to upgrade to a septic tank care system?"

I told this kid, who's younger than my toilet, that I wanted a system that would keep my wife from waking me up in the middle of the night to ask if I could hear the running drip.

He suggested the 400AK model, which fits most toilet tanks and should take an afternoon to replace.

I'd like to tell you it took just a few hours to install the 400AK. Tell you that my bathroom is silent and my jiggle-the-handle days are done.

I'd really like to tell you that.

But I'm still working out a few kinks.

Nothing big. Just the occasional drip.

I'm thinking it's the seal on the fill valve.

Might need to be replaced.

May 13, 2004

Outer beauty matters for a cool fridge

We recently remodeled our kitchen.

We changed the magnets on the refrigerator.

At least I still think it's our fridge. It's got two handles and we keep tossing food into it, which means it's either the fridge or we've added another teen to the house.

Of course the idea of a refrigerator being used to store cold food these days is really passé.

Seems the main reason for its centerpiece spot in our kitchen is so we can have a place to show off our magnets, and the revolving pieces of papers and photographs strategically placed under the magnets.

Who needs an office?

Pull up a chair to the fridge, plug in the laptop and you're golden. All your meetings and important papers, pictures of the kids ... and you don't have to get up for lunch.

It was nice showing off the kids' finger paintings. But now this wide-body appliance that makes ice and provides filtered water has become an expensive bulletin board.

Nothing gets put away. It gets put on the fridge.

We also have one of those handy magnetic boards with a marker, so you can leave important messages for the family. It's a can't miss, because you can't miss seeing the board.

I know the kids missed the note about shoveling snow. I wonder if they'll notice the reminder to clean their room.

The real job of our fridge magnets is to display holiday cards of friends and relatives posed in front of the Sears fireplace. Hey, love the relatives, but I don't think I look into my wife's eyes as much as I do her second cousins from Chicago.

Why must every need for milk turn into a trip down memory lane? And it's always the distant relatives, the ones you only see at weddings and funerals who send the pictures.

Couldn't tell you their names, but I can pick them out of a police lineup.

Since there's only so much prime eye-level fridge real estate to go around, we play a constant game of musical pictures for who gets the top spot: right side of fridge, just above the handle.

No one just has a magnet. Gone are the promos for pizza places or beauty salons.

Friends of ours have magnets in the exact shape and color of food. I suppose these are for folks who like to keep with a central theme. You put food inside the refrigerator, so why not have a fried egg, some fruity cereal or a bagel magnet out the outside.

Corny, but not as bad as those annoying magnets people stick on the fridge with stupid sayings from farm animals. A picture of a smiling pig says, "Pigs Are Friends, Not Food." Or a chicken includes the words, "Meat's No Treat For Those You Eat."

Aren't these animals squawking to the choir?

We're a society that wants more from our fridge magnets than just holding things up.

For just $10 a set, the fine folks at Fridge Fun will fill your appetite for knowl-edge with Word Magnets. You can create clever phrases, sentences, poems and messages by rearranging the magnetic word tiles, all while trying to decide if you want mayo or mustard with that sandwich.

What better place to expand one's vocabulary?

Or since you're just gonna stare at the refrigerator anyway, why not use the time to memorize fun magnetic quotes, like, "We're just bugs on the windshield of life!"

That'll keep food in the fridge.

My brother has magnets that make sounds. Press his telephone magnet and you hear a phone ring. Press his soda magnet and you hear a can popping open and the sound of soda filling a glass. Press his toilet bowl magnet and you hear ...

He doesn't have kids, so I guess he needs the artificial noise to break the si-lence.

I think my angst with the fridge magnets has to do with their placement. They're scattered all around, sending out negative vibes and creating bad karma.

It's time to bring the art of Feng Shui to our fridge. Create balance and har-mony with the magnets, offer purpose and prosperity.

Just as soon as I get rid of the pictures.

April 18, 2002

My junk drawer could be yours

For years we've collected junk.
Junk that's been used and abused, junk that's been wasted and junk that's been worn out.

Junk that was junk the day we got it and junk that became junk over time. Be it good junk or bad junk – all our junk ends up in one place: the junk drawer.

And nothing ever leaves the junk drawer.

Oh, I've tried to make junk drawer withdrawals, but I could never find the one junk drawer item I needed at that moment.

My wife is the curator of the junk drawer, and thus answers any search request with: "Did you look in the junk drawer?"

"Honey, I'm looking; it's not in the junk drawer."

Are you sure?" she'll ask. "I saw it in the junk drawer the other day."

"Well, it's not there now."

"Are you looking hard?"

I don't know what that means. Looking hard? I use both eyes and turn the lights on. I think that constitutes looking hard.

Fact is, there's nothing that we need in the junk drawer. Nothing I want. But maybe you want it?

It's yours. All of it. Take it.

Come on, you'll waste a full tank of gas driving around at these yard sales? I've got the same quality stuff in my junk drawer:

- A few of those plastic coin purses, the kind you squeeze at the ends to open. Got a green one from Penn's Woods Products with a picture of a turkey.
- A plastic mouth guard. It has some indents, but that shows durability.
- A pretty clean plastic retainer case.
- A Valentine's Day plastic decal of a cat.
- A very dried-out tube of Woltra Cocoa Butter Stik that helps speed the healing of damaged skin, smoothes blemishes and softens stretch marks.
- A dried out tube of Balloons in a Tube.
- A combination writing pad and year 2000 calendar from Ohio Technical College.
- I have those pads you put on the bottom of furniture to not scrape the floors. Some are felt, some plastic. None match, but who's gonna know?
- A deck of Tally-Ho playing cards without the six of clubs, queen of hearts and seven of hearts.

Eleven of those little golf pencils. I'll sell them as a set.

- A used mouthpiece to a baritone. It wasn't used as often as it should have been.

- An air-freshener holder, with some dried-up pieces of vanilla stuck inside.
- An open package of five-flavor LifeSavers.
- A package of heat-shrink electrical insulation.
- A container of Betta fish food pellets. It's a great deal. The fish lasted three days.
- A tattered 25-inch paper tape measure.
- An old VCR remote without batteries.
- A felt key holder from Gaslight Village in Lake George.
- Four very hard pieces of bubble gum.
- A solar-powered calculator that doesn't show the bottom half of the numbers.
- Some Christmas lights. Don't think they work.
- Three AAA batteries. Don't think they work.
- The plastic back that keeps batteries in a remote control.
- A handle to a piece of luggage.
- Some string, screws and rubber bands.
- A broken piece of plastic used to tack lights onto the eaves of the house.
- Instructions for changing the oil in a hurricane lamp.
- A bag of adhesive picture-hangers from Ames.
- A pack of 50-cent penny rolls and $10 quarter rolls.
- A compass that points southwest.
- Three-prong plug adapters.
- A red crayon. A die. A pipe cleaner.
- A 40 mm exposure roll of Fuji film, 24 mm Kodak film (I might get the rolls developed before selling).
- A film canister full of bent thumb tacks.
- One good clothespin and half of another.

If one man's junk is another man's treasure, let me offer you the opportunity to bask in the riches of a lifetime. Or maybe you see it as just fool's gold. Your call.

I just need to get junk out of the drawer.

June 02, 2005

We waste not, then want not

I don't want to say the leftovers in our refrigerator have aged, but General Tso was a corporal when we put a couple of pieces of his chicken inside it.

To be sure, this combination special has seen better days.

Like the day I brought it home. I think it was in June.

I'm not going out on a limb suggesting that anyone would miss my leftover General Tso combo.

Five pieces of hard chicken, sitting on an even harder bed of fried rice accompanied by an egg roll with vegetables growing from the inside out.

Even General Tso wouldn't go near the stuff. But still it sits in our fridge.

Just behind the tall glass of orange juice with just a sip left in it.

Right in front of the container with spaghetti, covered with meat sauce and peppers.

I think it's peppers.

I hope it's peppers.

And right next to the container with the cold piece of meatloaf that got a reprieve.

My wife wanted to throw the meatloaf out. Said it would just sit in the fridge. And sit in the fridge. And sit in the fridge. Said it happens all the time.

I swore, not this time.

"It tastes better the next day. When it's cold. Just leave it. I'll eat it."

And I will. Eventually.

So into the fridge goes Tupperware after Tupperware of extra burgers off the grill. Some drumsticks. A chunk of roast. A few slices of pizza. Tuna. Sauce. Soup. Baggies with salad. Sliced fruit. Diced vegetables.

I swear there's a jar of gefilte fish in there as old as the Last Supper. And I'm not talking about my last supper.

I just can't see throwing away good food. Unfortunately the good food turns bad because I can't see what leftovers we have.

There's more leftover food in the fridge than there is new food.

In theory, leftovers make sense. It means we're not wasting food. Eat some now … save some for later.

The problem in our house isn't with the leftover. It's with the meaning of "later."

We haven't really quantified how late later can be – or when it's too late.

Sometimes we remember to date the labels on the containers and bags. But I'm thinking of installing one of those odometer-style clocks, the kind used to count the world population and the U.S. debt. Open the fridge and watch the numbers tell you that leftover piece of chuck steak is getting older by the second.

I know the minute I start tossing stuff out is when someone wants to know what happened to the 2-month-old piece of chicken they were saving for dinner.

The thing about our leftovers is that we just can't bring ourselves to throw them out, even though we can no longer decipher what it is that we're saving.

I pulled something from the fridge the other day that resembled a piece of rock usually recovered by archeologists who chisel away at formations using little picks and hammers.

The only trace that it even came from this century was that it was sitting in a Tupperware container.

When I can no longer decide if it's animal or mineral I call out to my wife, the official arbiter in the Lewis house of when a leftover is no longer socially acceptable.

"Honey, what is this?" I ask, holding up the container, as if she were the Amazing Kreskin.

Nobel-winning scientists wouldn't have a clue, but my wife just squints at the specimen and makes a few educated guesses.

"Could be meatloaf. Could be tuna fish. Could be macaroni salad. Why don't you smell it?"

Do you get that a lot?

"Why don't you smell it?"

Now wouldn't you think that if two people can't identify leftover food by just looking at it, then smelling it might be a waste of time – not to mention a serious health risk?

At that point, I usually seek out a volunteer – always our family dog Boo Boo – who seems to know instantly that not only does the leftover no longer belong in the house, it might not be accepted at the town dump.

The good thing about having all this food is that we don't have to worry about going shopping.

This weekend, we're having leftovers. Could be meatloaf. Could be tuna. We're still not sure.

September 29, 2005

Flexibility is just a matter of time

I'm losing track of time.

That doesn't mean my days are moving too quickly or I'm moving too slowly.

I just can't keep track of time.

At least at home.

Never mind that we have at least two dozen timepieces. There are the clocks in the kitchen, the living room, the bedroom and the bathroom.

There are clocks on the microwave, on the stove and on the radio.

There's the television clock, VCR clock, DVD clock, not to mention the clock on the computer.

Time is not the problem. We have plenty of time.

What we don't have is the right time.

In the past month, we've lost power four times in our house.

Nothing major, but each outage meant we had to reset all the clocks. And then reset the clocks again. And again.

I don't know about you, but I just don't have the time to keep up with the time.

Even the answering machine tells us what time someone called. But when the power goes out, you have to reset the machine. I know this because I'm suddenly getting quite a few messages between midnight and 4 in the morning. So says our answering machine.

What we don't have in our house are two clocks with the same time. Not that I didn't try.

For the longest time, I was a diligent resetter.

The second the power returned, I'd scamper around the house to synchronize our life, reaching out to all digital objects.

But just when I finished setting one clock, I'd lose valuable seconds setting the next clock. So I'd run back to the clocks I reset first in hopes of bringing them up to time. But no matter how often I returned to reset, I always fell seconds short.

Then I got sloppy with the time.

While resetting the clocks, I'd mix up the PM with the AM, so at 6:30 at night we have bells going off, the radio coming on and the dog barking and scratching at the door because she thought it was time for her morning walk.

The only thing certain about time in our house is that we would have two minutes after the alarm sounds before the dog begins to pee on the floor.

Eventually, I began to improvise.

A couple of seconds here, a minute there, divide by two half-moons and carry over the leap year and I'd usually come within 30 to 40 minutes of the real time.

Unfortunately, because all the clocks are not set the same, every few minutes we have a different set of chimes going off. When one set of chimes ends, another begins.

Reminds me of when we sang "Row, row, row your boat" in camp. One person would start while the other person was in the middle of the song. It never ended. Same with the chimes. They never end.

As much as I have allowed time to run amuck in my house, I have taken what I believe is the appropriate steps to guarantee punctuality in the rest of my life.

I've set the clock in my car 22 minutes ahead.

Why? Ask anyone around here how long it takes to get from one place to an-ther, they'll tell you: 20 minutes. I added a little cushion for traffic.

Car clock reads 8:22 - that means it is really 8.

Car clock reads 8 - that means it is really 7:38.

It's a little game to keep the blood flowing.

If I get into my car in Liberty at 10:30, but the car clock reads 10:08, and a friend gets into his car at the exact same time in Monticello, how long will we sit in traffic on a Friday afternoon?

Of course, none of this matters if I go by the time on my watch, which I have set for seven minutes ahead of what is the actual time - not to be confused with the time on my car clock or any timepiece in my house.

A few of you might wonder why I just don't set all the clocks in my life at the same, correct time and just leave myself plenty of time to get where I want to go.

I would. But in a couple of weeks, we'll have daylight-saving time. While every-one tries to figure out how to reset their lives - do I gain an hour, lose an hour, owe somebody an hour - I know I'm set.

I created our own flex time.

So when the kids ask what time is it, I ask them what time do they want? Give me a minute, and I'll find them a clock with that time.

March 16, 2006

In sickness, health and a dead mouse

We had an unwelcome visitor surprise us during the Thanksgiving holiday.

A small, beady-eyed hairy sort with tiny ears, a twitching nose and an unabashed eagerness to sleep just about anywhere and eat whatever crumbs we had in the house.

While that might describe several of my relatives and an uncle on my wife's side, the truth is that our unexpected houseguest was not a person. We had a mouse.

I know the mouse was not welcome in our house because my wife, usually a loving soul with a heart of gold, said I had to kill it. She never suggests that we kill any of my relatives. Even the uninvited ones. At least not out loud.

Not that we ever encourage them to come into the house. I'm still talking about the mice.

Like having a backed-up septic system and a dry well, an occasional rodent seeking warmth in your home during the winter months is just one of the perks of living in the country.

Every time Bonnie hears little feet scampering in the walls, sees droppings in the basement or catches one scurrying past, she morphs from mild-mannered mom into Lizzie Borden crying out for blood. Only she doesn't want any of it on her hands.

"You've got to set the traps and kill it!"

I appreciate the confidence she has in me to get into killer mode. It takes quite a bit of imagination. But you'd think after 25 years of marriage, she'd know my response.

"Why can't you kill it?" I reply, recognizing that my wife has the ability, skill and courage to handle such a task.

I lack all three.

"Killing the mouse is your job," she says, as if, had I taken the time to read the fine print on our marriage license, I would have known that. It's right there, clear as day between early-morning dog walker and last-minute milk buyer. Under husband jobs: mouse killer.

Let me go on record to say that I'm not a fan of mice. Excluding Mickey, Minnie and Mighty, I've never had much use for them. I'm especially bothered by the unwelcome houseguest variety.

My problem is you just can't shoo out a mouse.

My other problem is that I'm not good with dead things. That encompasses everything from actually doing something that will make a thing dead (i.e., killing it) to ultimately discarding said dead thing (i.e., getting rid of the thing that I've killed).

Over the years, I've decided to take a few measures in order to follow through on my vows to love, cherish and kill and discard an unwanted mouse.

Truth is, catching an unwanted mouse is easy. Put a little dab of peanut butter on the old spring-loaded Victor trap and just wait. We don't need better mouse traps. Just better-tasting peanut butter.

I'm sure the mouse would argue, if it could, that this is not the healthiest diet. And advocates for the rights of rodents (you know there must be some kind of group out there) would protest such a brutal death.

To those folks, I say, with little empathy, "Let me bring the mice to your place!"

I can't do much about our dirty kids, but a dirty rodent has no place in our home. Not intentionally.

Until the day I hear one cry out with a mouth full of peanut butter, "What about some jelly!" I'm taking them down. Taking them out of the house is another question.

You can call me the queasy executioner.

Armed with my son's long snowmobile gloves, goggles (strictly precautionary) and an extra-long screwdriver, I carefully flick the trap onto a snow shovel. Then, with my arms extended, I walk the long green mile to the woods — careful never to look directly at the trap.

First time Bonnie saw my outfit, she wondered if I was getting rid of a mouse or plutonium.

"Should we start packing?"

"These things carry diseases," I said.

"Superman gets closer to Kryptonite."

"It could bite."

"In its dreams. I think it took its last bite."

I flicked off the mouse and set up a new trap. I'm sure others will follow. It's getting cold. I'm keeping the gloves and goggles close by.

November 29, 2007

Barry's Bucolic Life in the Country

Spring cleanup can drain the fun out of a weekend

The ebb and flow of my life in rural Sullivan County reached a watermark of sorts this past weekend as I tried to rid myself of a pair of old toilet bowls and a swamp on my front lawn.

And people say country folks don't know how to live.

Eliminating the water-holding toilets and the water-holding swamp had less to do with coincidence and more with the annual convergence of cleansing our home and our land of unwanted items.

It's the seasonal solstice known around these parts as spring cleanup.

I consider it one of those special perks of living in the country that generally goes unheralded the rest of the year.

Sadly, I suspect it's not even on the top 10 list of questions on the inquiring minds of most potential home buyers.

People ask about schools.

Realtors talk up low taxes and quiet neighbors.

How far is the market? Where's the park? What's the traffic like?

No one ever asks about the quality of a town's spring cleanup.

How many times a year? What do they take? Can you pick up as well as drop off?

Inconsequential? Maybe.

But after replacing two toilet bowls and having them sit in my basement all winter, I cared less about the park in my town and more about the fact that I live in a place that will give me a place other than my basement to park these toilets.

I suppose if you've spent your whole life in the country, then spring cleanup and toilet-bowl trash sort of loses its luster.

We moved out of our Brooklyn apartment when I was still in my teens, so I never really gave much thought to how a person disposes of a toilet bowl.

The common answer might be to just leave it out on the street, but even in a city, where you see just about everything, you really don't see too many toilets out on the curb.

No such worries when living in the country.

We may lack public transportation, a major shopping mall and decent cell phone service, but I've got a town dump that, during spring cleanup, welcomed my old toilets with open arms.

Turns out ridding myself of two worthless toilets was easy.

Ridding my lawn of a swamp that, in time, had taken on the physical characteristics of the Everglades was bit more of a challenge.

Personally, I thought the swamp gave the lawn a tropical feel that I'm sure plenty of folks in Westchester County or Connecticut would pay good money to have on their property.

Much better than one of those lawn ornaments where it looks like water is magically coming out of a faucet that's not attached to anything.

That you can buy. But a swamp - that's priceless.

I tried telling that to my wife, but she wasn't buying it. At any price.

I was hoping spring cleanup would extend to just ridding our basement of the old toilets and allow nature to take its course outside.

Who was I to disturb the circle of life?

Her cleanup plan was for me to fill in the swamp and cart away the mounds of old leaves so we can extend our lawn.

For 20 years, I've been extending my lawn. You know what you get when you extend your lawn - more lawn to take care of and more lawn to extend. Doesn't stop.

That's when it occurred to me - the uncanny similarities between having children and having a lawn.

I'm constantly picking up after both.

I'm forever throwing money at both.

Every year, the boys grow, and so does my lawn.

And my wife critiques my handling of both.

I looked at my swamp that needed to be covered and the leaves that covered my lawn. Then I looked at my watch and figured out how much more of my weekend I'd be wasting carting leaves into the woods, not to mention cleaning the swamp.

I'm proud to say the leaves are off the lawn and you can't see the swamp. I'm not done, but that's OK. At least the toilets are gone.

May 04, 2006

I'm attached to lawn chairs

My boys say we need to get new folding lawn chairs because our old ones don't have cup holders.

And, they add, we're missing the carrying case.

The poor souls. How did they ever last this long?

"Of course we need new chairs," I said, standing in a pool of my own sarcasm.

I reminded them that the actual seat in our folding chairs, which I always took to be the key component in the chair, was still functioning properly.

And I noted, not having a cup holder did not really prevent them from having a cup in the chair. They still had the freedom of choice to either hold their drink – or place it on the ground.

As for the carrying case, that was really more their problem, since we always considered the boys to be our personal carrying case.

Even without a cup holder and the missing carrying case, the folding chairs I take from the shed every spring are still light years ahead of the ugly aluminum, webbed monsters that my brothers and I schlepped across the hot sands of Brighten Beach.

So, what's up with these cup holders?

When did we all get so thirsty that we can't sit anywhere unless there's at least one cup holder by our side?

Or so lazy that we can't imagine bending down to place our drink on the ground?

And we can't carry lawn chairs without a carrying case?

Are we never satisfied?

Apparently chairs that simply hold our derrieres will no longer suffice.

They must also hold our drinks.

I would have killed for the chance to sit in a high-tech, forest green, form fitting model with durable webbing that can easily be folded with the tug of just one hand.

And carried over my shoulder.

We didn't have any stink'n reinforced models with two layers of polyester fabric, custom contoured grommets and shoulder straps. The chairs of my youth were made of an alloy that would bend when you just looked at it funny.

When you looked at our chairs you couldn't help but laugh.

Instead of picking out solid color webbing, my family went with what could best be described as a bad Hawaiian shirt.

The only bright spot was that we always stood out in a sea of beachgoers.

There was no concern about cup holders at the end of the armrests, just the fear that the sharp metal at the end of the rests would slice an arm if waved close to them.

And there was the seat – although we never really sat completely in the seat. You tried to sit, but you usually wound up sinking between the webbing, while the other half of your bottom would teeter on the edge of frayed cloth.

I swear, the webbing on these things would fray from the fresh air.

Fray is the critical word. You see, the webbing would never completely tear. Just fray.

A complete tear would give you reason to throw the chair out. But with a good fray, men across this land could show off their fix-it skills.

Men with real common sense would just go out and buy a new chair. Men with less common sense would buy a repair kit and spend hours replacing the webbing.

Then there was my grandfather, who would use electrical tape to reinforce the webbing.

The combination of the hot sun, my sweaty thighs and the adhesive from the ends of the tape would create an unusually strong bond that would have me trapped in the seat for hours.

When it was time to leave the beach I'd stand, still sticking to the chair. I'd close my eyes and brace myself while my mother would pull on the chair, freeing me not only of the seat but from several layers of skin.

So, I'll go to the shed and take out chairs without cup holders and carrying cases. It could be worse. I could be taking out the electrical tape.

May 26, 2005

Barry: Weeds need whacking? Barry's your hit man

I'll admit that I don't know much about gardening. Couldn't pick out a smokewood from a sneezewort or a crocus from a ficus.

What's the difference between a creeping gloxinia, a bloody cranesbill and a wonga-wonga vine? I haven't a clue. They could be Ben & Jerry rejects or the opening act for Metallica. Truth is, I had to look those names up.

What do you expect from a guy who spent his formative years tending to a stoop instead of a shrub?

But, given all that, folks, if you're looking for someone this summer to whack your weeds — go no further. I'm your guy.

Consider me the Tony Soprano of Weedwackers.

Any weed that messes with me will be pushing up daisies.

I cut first and ask questions later.

Questions like, should I really have cut that? Was that a weed? Am I in trouble now?

If you have to ask — you're in trouble.

OK, sometimes I get a bit carried away and start playing executioner with our ferns. At least I think they're ferns. Well, they were our ferns. I hope they'll grow back. If they don't, well, you really can't blame me.

Nobody ever said lawn care was pretty.

Does it mean from time to time I might have to spill a little oil?

Accidentally take the life of an unsuspecting morning glory or a snoozing Siberian iris in order to whack away some troublesome weeds?

I take no pleasure clipping a tulip. Not really. But after I fertilize, herbicide and try a little nitrocide, after I've laid enough lime to mark every ball field in the country, I'm ready to kick some grass.

Put a John Deere XT250BLE in my hands with an anti-vibration front, overmolded throttle and 17-inch cutting swath and you're practically giving me a license to kill. Or at the very least tame the worst dandelion.

Kinda sound like Tony, don't I?

There's a sense of power, freedom and entitlement that comes with swinging a Weedwacker that you just don't get sitting or pushing a mower. No confined spaces. No getting stuck in the mud. No worrying about hitting a rock to get those low-lying weeds. You want to hit a rock.

Whack! Whack! Whack!

Teach it a lesson for trying to hide those weeds.

Whack! Whack! Whack!

You never saw squirrels run so fast. It'll be a long time before they try to sneak into my bird feeder.

Whhhrrrrr!

Try doing that with your riding mower.

You have to cut in rows. Circle the beds. Check the height of the blade. Keep emptying the bags.

They're nothing but golf carts with fancy blades. The new ones have massage seats, cup holders and surround sound.

Are you cutting grass or teeing off?

You don't even need your hands on a mower. I've got a neighbor who chows down a sandwich while steering with his knees. Shift into low and you can check e-mail on your BlackBerry.

Take your hand off the John Deere XT250BLE and you won't have to worry about those hairy legs any longer.

Sneeze and you'll give yourself a bikini wax you'll never forget.

Look, it's a jungle out there. Or if I'm not out there, it'll quickly turn into a jungle.

So you can either sit around twiddling your green thumbs waiting for some organic liquid fertilizer to travel to your plant's roots so it can defend itself, moving with all the speed of an overheated Chevy trying to make it up Wurtsboro Mountain on a late Friday afternoon in the summer — or you can give me a shout.

No big deal.

I come over ... put on my goggles ...turn up the throttle on the John Deere XT250BLE ... and badda boom, badda bing ... problem gone.

Someone asks about your weeds, you tell them, "I called Barry and fuhgedaboutit."

May 31, 2007

Keeping Bambi away with that urine fragrance

I love living in the country. So safe. So quiet. So full of fresh air.

As long as you don't mind the constant threat of bears, attacking mosquitoes, howling dogs, screeching bobcats and the fresh fragrance of urine that we spray on our fresh-smelling flowers to ward off deer.

Who knew getting close to nature could be so dangerous?

My wife said we have to spray to keep Bambi away from the house. I told her if she keeps using that god-awful urine, she'll keep Barry away from the house.

I'm worried that's the plan.

"Honey, we paid an awful lot of money for these flowers. Do we really want our garden to smell like the men's room at the Port Authority?"

She argues that if we don't spray the deer repellent, they'd eat us out of hosta and home, and finish off our lilies and aborvitae for dessert.

So we've spread what's called Liquid Fence, a biodegradable, rain-resistant spray with an admittedly "pungent" odor that promises to keep our garden free of unwanted critters.

To be honest, I'm less concerned about the eating habits of the neighborhood deer and more worried that we'll be responsible for the sudden and tragic deaths of our newspaper carrier and mailman once they get within 500 feet of our "pungent" Liquid Fence.

My wife calls it the "smelly" deer repellent.

Smelly to me is the bottom of a diaper pail. That block of cheese you left on the counter for three days. For some unknown reason, my son's car. That's smelly.

This stuff would make a skunk tear up.

You want to draw bin Laden out of the cave? Fire off some deer repellent.

They could market this stuff to not only ward off deer, but cat burglars, trick-or-treaters and those pesky people who interrupt my dinner to want to know if I've found peace with the Lord. I promise you, one whiff and they'll be doing a whole lot of praying.

The only thing worse than having the urine smell is that we PAY to have the urine smell — which gives further credence to the notion that us baby boomers will do just about anything to get rid of our money. After buying pet rocks, bottled water and television we can get over the air for free, it makes sense that we'd pay for animal urine.

My wife contends the "repellent" is perfectly safe for the environment. This, from the same person who when we went camping, wouldn't let the boys tinkle in the woods because it might harm the plants.

But now we buy urine with a smell so potent that it could knock out an entire herd of wild boar just to keep deer away from our day lilies. Buy urine? I've got three boys and a dog who wouldn't need much convincing to water the plants. They'd be relieved.

Fine, we get rid of the deer. Now if only they made urine that would keep away mosquitoes.

Someone has.

Seems those busy folks at PredatorPee, the same ones who brought you CoyotePee, FoxPee, BobcatPee, WolfPee and Mt.LionPee having been working overtime in their labs up in Bangor, Maine, (I suppose it's a way to stay both busy and warm in Bangor, Maine,) to create NoSkeeto, guaranteed to keep those pesky mosquitoes away from your lawn, your pets or your kids.

For just $15.99, you can get 12 ounces of this stuff.

That might seem a bit steep at first, but consider the man-hours associated with trying to get the cup in just the right spot.

If you're like me, and you're not sure which urine to choose, you can always pick up the PredatorPee Sampler, a handy five-bottle set that matches just the right urine to your needs.

Or, you can put up a real 8-foot fence to keep the deer out and just stay inside, safe from the bugs and the bears and bobcats and enjoy nature the way God intended, with air conditioning and cable TV.

August 03, 2006

The penny social:
a time-honored and secret event

I never thought I'd get so excited for the chance to win a My Little Pony eraser set.

But I wanted it.

And I wanted to win the microwave potato-chip maker, the 1,000-piece ladybug puzzle and the tacky plastic Christmas place mats.

I also wanted to win the set-of-four Teddy bear mugs, the dozen chocolate cupcakes and the Santa Claus jelly-bean holder.

I wanted to win them all.

But it wouldn't be easy.

I was up against 200 other men, women and children who squeezed into our school cafeteria on a cold winter night in Grahamsville for a much anticipated and apparently highly competitive event known as the penny social.

Having never attended a penny social, I was taken aback by two long-standing traditions: It really only costs a penny a ticket, and it really is a social event.

Especially on a cold winter night in Grahamsville.

There's also a third and even more important tradition that only aficionados of penny socials know: When they say doors open at 5:30 p.m. and the calling begins at 7, you better be on line no later than 5.

Or you might run out of time to survey and bid on all the prizes. And that's what a penny social is really all about. The prizes.

Oh, you'll meet friends and neighbors and exchange pleasantries about the weather and kids. But all niceties are tossed aside when you're competing mano a mano for the chance at Christmas doggie socks, a pair of those round rubber things that opens jars and a set of business fax cover sheets.

It's like having free reign at the dollar store.

A penny social is sort of like a combination silent auction, flea market and bingo. Sort of.

For $2, I got three sets of tickets, each with 25 chances, three chances at a door prize and a cup of coffee or fruit punch and either cookies or a piece of cake.

Who needs Vegas?

Once I bought my tickets for the fundraiser for two honorable groups - the Tri-Valley chapter of the Future Business Leaders of America and the Grahamsville Fire Department's Ladies Auxiliary - I entered a cafeteria packed with people trying to make their way along 200 chairs surrounding a few dozen long tables, every inch occupied with items donated by community sponsors that, well - let's just call it stuff

Times Herald-Record photo by Dominick Fiorille

I wish the bunny feet came with a shoe horn.

Best holiday to be a bunny

8:40 a.m.: Who wouldn't want to be the Easter Bunny?

The Easter Bunny!

You don't have the Santa problems, dealing with pushy parents who don't want you to promise their kids anything and their kids who want you to get them everything — all the while you Ho! Ho! Ho! till you're blue blue blue.

No such problems for the Easter Bunny.

No one asks you for anything. Not even an egg.

Wear a cute costume, sit on cushy egg-shaped yellow throne and don't say a word.

Shake a kid's hand. Pat a head. Maybe hop.

That's what I thought driving March 14 to the Galleria at Crystal Run, after finally negotiating with the mall folks and officials at Instant Photo Corp. of America to allow me to be their bunny.

You think it's tough getting through customs at the airport? Try getting clearance to be a mall Easter Bunny.

9:30: Stefanie Moronio, the local manager of the Bunny & Me photo booth, leads me through the bowels of the Galleria so I can change into my bunny suit.

Here's the deal with the suit. If you have a fear of looking funny in public, being in a confined space or getting close to germs, don't get in the suit.

They hire nine mall bunnies who over the month share two suits (one large and one medium), two pairs of bunny feet but just one bunny head.

No dry cleaning the suits. They're turned inside out to air dry.

I luck out being first bunny of the day.

That means I don't have to breath in the smell from the other bunnies (nothing personal). Stefanie pulls out a can of Lysol spray to eliminate the germs.

Warning to aspiring bunnies: Be careful. Take in too many whiffs of Lysol and you think you really are the Easter Bunny.

Stefanie says it's easier to breath while wearing the head now that they've taken away the black screen from in front of the mouth.

The screen is still in front of the eyes so you don't see them in the pictures. Remember the movie "The Fly" and what the fly sees trying to look out? Same thing.

On the way, she reminds me of the two big rules: be mindful where you put your bunny hands and no talking.

9:50: Waiting at the set for the mall to open, I ask Stefanie: What do you tell a bunny who has to go to the bathroom?

"We tell them not to think about it."

I'm so glad I didn't have a second cup of coffee. But my nose really itches.

Stefanie reminds me again — "No talking." Boy, these IPCA folks really do a good job vetting a person.

10:00: I'm on. A few stroller walkers stop so their kids can see the Easter Bunny. I slowly dance over to one not-so-sure little girl. Mom lifts out her 6-month-old.

"Oh, look at the Easter Bunny. You wanna say hi? Say, 'Hi Easter Bunny. Hiiii.'"

She's still clutching Mom.

I might be minutes into the job, but 22 years of parenting, three children and dozens of trips to theme parks have taught me how close a 6-foot-3 Easter Bunny can get to a toddler before traumatizing them for life.

I tickle the baby's stomach and she laughs.

10:08: I'm a hit with the kids.

Two-year-old Kayden Taliaferro of Milford, Pa., gives me the once over.

I give Kayden my very special Easter Bunny dance — a combination of Chubby Checker doing the Twist, John Travolta at the disco and Groucho Marx in "Horse Feathers."

I get a big hug.

10:25: My nose itches, sweat is getting in my eyes and still no photo customers. But I'm having a ball.

I wave at everyone and everyone smiles and waves back at the Easter Bunny.

Now I know how the folks wearing Mickey, Donald and Goofy must feel.

One man walking with his wife shakes his finger at me, smiles and says I forgot him last year. Cute.

A kid trailing his mom gets upset because she won't stop to let him see the Easter Bunny. She says later and tells him to keep up.

He walks, all the while looking back at me.

I wave bye to the boy.

Upset, he waves back.

Note to parents: When your child wants to visit the Easter Bunny at the mall, let them. You'll never forget their smile during those few minutes.

You'll want to remember it, because in about 10 years the last place they'll want to walk with you is the mall.

10:40: My first photo customer.

Stefanie walks Ben Ferrier, 3, of Walden, into my gated Easter Bunny kingdom, right between Cohen's Optical and Whitehall Jewelers.

As she positions him on my lap, I want to say hello, wish him a happy Easter and ask if he's been a good boy — say something to the kid.

Stefanie seems to sense my anxiety and tells Ben to say "hi" to the Easter Bunny. Then she gives me a look that reminds me of the two big rules.

"Look here and smile!" Stefanie yells to us.

Ben smiles. I smile.

Why I am smiling? No one can see my face.

"One more time! Smile!"

Again, I smile.

11:00: My second and last photo customer.

I can't help smiling for the picture. Maybe it's the suit.

With their paid pictures (various packages of 5x7s, 3x5s or wallets) folks get a free plastic Jell-O Egg Jiggler.

Our shot looks great. Nice keepsake. We're both smiling.

11:15: Stefanie takes me back to change.

You want to lose weight? Forget Jenny Craig. Put on this suit for an hour.

I'm drenched.

Robert Schulman, 21, of Port Jervis, is the next bunny. He opts for the medium suit and sprays the head.

I suggest he Lysol twice.

He wears an iPod under the suit. He says the music helps him dance and keeps time moving.

I didn't need a stink'n iPod.

These kids today.

11:35: I watch Robert for a few minutes. Not bad, but I can tell he doesn't have his own kids. It should be mandatory.

As I walk to get a smoothie, I hear a mom yell, "Look, there's the Easter Bunny."

I turn around and smile.

She's pointing to Robert.

Guess it's true. The suit does make the bunny.

March 23, 2008

DANIEL JOSEPH SMYTHE 2003

June Cleaver?
No, but still damn good

My mom tells us that she's got a new burial plot in Jersey to save us from having to drive out to Long Island to visit her.

"I knew if I stayed there, you'd never visit. I wanted to make your life easier when I'm dead. So how are the boys?"

I'd love to see Hallmark put this touching scene on a Mother's Day card.

By the way, Mom's feeling fine.

Oh, she has the typical emphysema that comes with 40 years of tar and nicotine, a heart that sometimes needs a push from a Duracell and bones that not only feel an impending storm but can provide the barometric pressure.

She's got aches and pains, and I swear she's shrinking. One day I'll go see her and there'll be nothing but red hair and a pair of slippers.

But thank God, she's not dying.

I couldn't take the guilt.

And I think she has too much pleasure dishing it out.

In some ways it's what keeps her going.

The effectiveness of Mom's guilt is tied directly to the fact that she operates without any pretense of shame. Or sleight of hand.

She once called to ask if there was anything wrong with my fingers?

"No, why do you ask?"

"I figured your fingers weren't working, and that's why you couldn't dial the phone to find out how I'm doing."

Think of it as Koufax throwing a fastball. Koufax is gonna throw the heat. The batter knows the heat is coming. But no matter how he sets up in the batters box ... when the ball comes, you're gonna miss it.

I know what Mom's about to throw my way, and I still strike out every time.

It's the rookies – sales clerks, waiters, children – that never even see it coming.

When we walk into a store, I actually feel a bit sorry for the sales clerks. If they only knew.

"My son came down from the country and he needs to get a TV. Your flier says you have sets on sale. What's on sale?"

I start to wander off.

I'm embarrassed. She's warming up.

"I'm sorry, the sale starts tomorrow. That's when the prices will be reduced."

"Yea, but my son's here today. He's not coming back tomorrow. He needs a TV. They may buy two. What's on sale?"

"Ma, it's OK. The sale starts tomorrow. We'll wait. It's OK. Really. Let's go."

She can't hear me. Like Jordan on the foul line or Tiger on the green, she can block out the crowds.

She stares down the salesman.

"I'm not coming back tomorrow."

It's sad to see a grown man wilt.

"OK ... what kind of set are you looking for?"

I want to leave the store. Maybe the state. But I'll leave with a bargain only Mom could buy.

I suppose there's a June Cleaver out there somewhere.

A mom who gets up before dawn to have a nutritious breakfast ready for her family, who sets out a tray of brownies for an after-school snack and always has a roast warming in the oven.

I just know she's not living in an apartment in Brooklyn.

In our house, Mom's balanced breakfast was to make sure there was an equal distribution of milk and cold cereal. There was change set out on a tray for ice cream and the oven was warmed for our TV dinners.

On pasta night we had ketchup instead of sauce. Dessert was Entenmann's.

But that's OK. Mom didn't do gourmet.

Instead she kept three city boys on the straight and narrow.

She puts up with a wise-ass son who never stops marveling at her wit, wisdom and backbone. She's a fighter.

She didn't spare the rod. She didn't always spoil the child.

But she taught us right from wrong. How to respect others. How to act like a man.

She helped me fill out the checklist on my baseball cards.

She never threw out my cards.

And she got a plot in Jersey. Just to save us a long drive to Long Island.

Damn she's good.

May 08, 2003

Gritty grill
holds treats for everyone

Pssst.

Hey guy ... come here.

So, you gonna have a big holiday weekend bash? Play Martha Stewart to the in-laws, your wife's sister from Jersey, her accountant husband and their two kids.

Real fancy schmancy.

Two different kinds of potato salad, the good baked beans and spicy brown mustard.

Gonna fire up the grill, aren't ya?

Let me give you a few tips.

You won't see these on Emeril. The Iron Chefs ... they don't have a clue. That Puck guy only wishes he had the nerve.

Ya' listening?

Don't clean the grill.

I'm not talking about dusting away the winter cobwebs. I mean leave the grit on the grates.

If you leave it they will eat.

Doesn't matter if it's cast iron, porcelain-enameled or stainless steel.

The thing that comes between the charcoals and your food should have history. A sense of place. Not a shine from Easy Off.

Push the button on the crossover ignition system and you set in motion a 75,000 BTU per hour input that will not only grill your "spicy beef satay" to juicy perfection, but also provide enough power to jettison a two-man lunar module.

Your eyes widen, watching as flames reach up and smack around the grate.

Like some mad scientist who brings the monster back to life, you marvel at the rejuvenation of past grilling conquests.

The family thinks they're having "shrimp with coconut milk curry" but they keep smelling last summer's "pork ribs with spiced apple-cider mop."

Or could it be the aroma of "Arabian nights grilled herbed chicken?"

Hey, we ate that years ago.

They sure did.

But no good chef reveals his secrets.

You just stand over the grill wearing a cotton twill apron and a Cheshire cat smile, holding a set of tongs and a Sam Adams, getting pleasure from the memories being spawned off your gritty grill.

You know full well that new brass bristled brush with the notched scraper the wife bought will never get near the decades-old clump of – well, who knows what – that has cocooned on the grate.

Imagine a grilled smorgasbord each time you fire the thing up.

You fancy a filet, the wife has a hankering for haddock and the kids are clamoring for chicken. But why buy three different dishes?

Grill long enough, and each dish will smell and taste like the meal before. And before that. And before that.

Everybody gets what they want all the time.

It's a good thing.

Now that you're bold enough not to brush, you'll want to know when to put the food on the grill.

The grate has got to be hot. But how do you know when it's hot enough?

Some folks might suggest a dual-purpose thermometer.

A toy for amateurs.

I traditionally go with the singe method.

Light the grill and close the lid.

Wait a few minutes and then open.

If the heat burns the hair off your hands, you got a ways to go. Lose the forearm hair and you can take the marinated meat out of the fridge.

When the eyebrows are gone, you're ready to grill.

At this point the leftover marinade not only adds flavor to the meat, but coats and soothes your second degree burns.

So let's review. Don't clean the grill and be man enough to lose your hair.

Now you can take food orders. Just write down what they want and nod your head in agreement. It won't matter. It'll all taste like steakchickenfish.

And that's a good thing.

May 24, 2002

Barry gives birth to a loaf of life

A guy walks into a temple and tells 20 Jewish women he's got no dough but he's ready to bake some challah.

Stop me if you've heard this one.

But seriously, folks.

Ever since last summer, when I went "in the back" at Gombo's Bakery in South Fallsburg to watch the making of challah, the traditional Jewish bread, I longed for the chance to create my own loaf.

Not just to buy as I had in the past but to bake.

To combine with my own two hands the flour, yeast, water and eggs, to balance the standard ingredients with my personal favorites so that I might beat and braid and baste and bake and ever so carefully lightly brown my edible work of art. To give life to a challah.

Like snowflakes, each loaf is different; just the manual twisting and tucking of the dough, a simplistic, delicious masterpiece.

Let the masses pick off the supermarket and bakery shelves. Not that there's anything wrong with that.

But why settle for store-bought when in the confines of my own kitchen I could provide the Lewis family with a true, homemade challah.

I imagine no better way to celebrate Rosh Hashana, the Jewish New Year that begins tomorrow night at sundown, than with my own baked creation.

But how? An old-time miracle?

Better yet, a class in the art of challah making.

This brings us back to those 20 Jewish women, members of the Catskill region of Hadassah who gathered last week at Congregation Ahavath Israel in Liberty for the challah class.

Educational and informative? Very. A good time had by all? Absolutely. Long? I did mention we had 20 Jewish women in the room.

"Ladies, it'll be a late night if we don't start cooking," tactfully warned class-organizer Brenda Stieffel Sherman of Liberty, breaking up the impromptu chat session for some much-needed kneading.

I teamed with Debbie Glatt of Monticello, who volunteered me to knead as she didn't want to get her jewelry dirty. I used two hands to pound our dough into a pulp.

"I don't think we'll be putting any bakeries out of business," she said.

"Knead it like a baby — if you're not careful, it won't rise," said another.

The women were getting vicious.

"You're only supposed to use one hand to knead," said Judy Goldman, our class instructor, looking down at my two dough-sticky hands. "You knead with your right and keep your left hand clean for turning the bowl and adding ingredients."

I watched one woman knead to perfection. With one hand.

"She runs a bakery in Swan Lake," shouted another woman.

A challah ringer.

I shoved both hands back into the bowl.

More flour. More water. More vanilla. More mess.

More than two hours after we first began our challah class, it was finally time to let our dough rise.

The husbands returned to pick up their wives:

"Are you done?"

The women cried out, "Our dough is rising!"

The men were unnerved: "The sun'll be rising. Come on!"

Another hour passed. Time to braid the challah.

I remember watching the men at Gumbo's braid, flipping the dough like they were dealers in Vegas. Divide the dough into thirds. Long snakes.

Over, over, over, pinch, tuck over, over, over, pinch, tuck. I couldn't tie my shoes that fast.

The bakery lady was braiding her third loaf. I was having trouble with my slip knot.

"Braid the dough like you braid your daughter's hair," yelled someone in the back.

These women are ruthless.

Why did I have three sons? One daughter, and I could have made the perfect challah. I still needed to baste.

Debbie said I could take our challah home to bake. In fact, she insisted. It was midnight when I took the challah out of my oven. A round loaf. Lightly browned.

The boys asked for a piece. I gave them a look.

"Cut my baby?"

They gave me a look.

Tomorrow. We'll eat it tomorrow.

September 21, 2006

A Halloween treat: end of the candy run

The Goobers gravy train has come to a screeching halt.

The Butterfingers bonanza is busted.

My boys, who just yesterday favored M&Ms are now teens whose tastes favor Eminem.

While ghosts and goblins and pint-sized Spider-Mans are out tonight peddling tricks for treats, my gang will all be home helping hand out the goodies.

They've reached the age when Halloween becomes a spectator sport.

I'm not shedding any tears, but exhaling a sigh of relief. As they say in the costumed candy game, it was a good run.

For the boys it was a good ride.

Free food. Some loose change. The only heavy lifting was their fingers on the door bell.

But for us trick-or-treat chauffeurs, the yearly road trip for hours and hours around and the countryside was a journey into the don't-get-comfortable zone.

In Brooklyn, my parents had it easy. They just said be careful and don't get home late.

We went right for the apartments.

Heat. Elevators. Six stories high and six apartments on each floor. You do the math.

Living in the sticks – where you're a stone's throw away from just another stone – the trick was getting the kids in and out and in and out and in and out of the car enough times so they'd arrive home with enough treats.

And doing so without them noticing you pilfering their candy-corn bags.

To me, Halloween's a test in time management.

You have a definitive goal: get goodies.

A finite resource: a willing parent.

A subject: homes willing to give goodies.

An objective: getting parents to drive to get the goodies.

And obstacles: Think it's easy to strap a lion in a car seat 30 times and not crease its tail or damage its mane?

Drive to a house. Get out. Get the boys out of their car seats. Walk them up to the house. They ring the bell. Get a Mounds. Walk back to the car. Back into the car seat. Back out of the driveway and down the road to another house.

"Save the Mounds," I'd yell, watching in the rearview as they upholster the seats in chocolate.

"It's your third Mounds. And you just had a Reese's. Did you eat a Milky Way? You don't need another Mounds."

By this point they've got enough sugar in them to push the car to the next house.

"No you can't eat the apple. We don't know what's in the apple. I didn't say something was in the apple. No, I don't think your aunt put anything in the apple."

"Hurry up and finish the Mounds. Time for more trick-or-treat. Wipe your face. Not on the seats!"

Can you feel the time-management stress?

So folks, I'm begginya, don't make it worse.

Speaking as a consultant – no longer an active participant, I'd like to offer some tips that'll keep the kids moving:

I'm always impressed with people who take time to make up bags. Must be the same folks who start their holiday shopping in the spring.

And they always have the bags by the door.

You ring. They open.

Kids give a quick "trick-or-treat."

Folks drop in a bag of goodies.

"Thank you."

"Welcome."

Outta there.

No chitchat.

None of this, "And what are you supposed to be?" Or, "Honey, you gotta come here and see this."

I'm sorry, but you're probably house 37 out of 53. You know how many times that car seat went up and down before we got to your doorbell?

Not even the supersize Snickers will move this gang of ghosts.

Keep the menu simple. Just wrapped candy. No apples. No pies. No chocolate chip cookies.

Don't you read the papers?

Look, I'd love to chat, but the kids are already at the door.

"Hey, let me guess ... three SpongeBob SquarePants and a Powerpuff Girl. Right? Honey, come here, you gotta see this. Get the camera and bring those apples. Hey, kids, you forgot your apples!"

October 31, 2002

Happy Turkey Day!
Put a lid on it, will ya?

Later today our family will travel over the river and through the woods to grandma's house.
Actually we just go up the hill to my mother-in-law's, but I'm trying to create some holiday mood.

But before we go, my wife will ask if I have everything.

She's not talking about bringing the wine. Not worried that I might forget the dessert. Isn't the slightest bit concerned that we might somehow leave without the boys.

I know what she means by "everything" and she knows what she means by "everything."

Everything means containers and lids.

Not that we've forgotten the true meaning of Thanksgiving.

Oh sure, we're thankful for the good health of our family and friends.

Thankful for the time we can all spend together.

Thankful for the bounty of good harvest (sorry, it's that holiday spirit again).

But let's be honest as we start loosening up the notches on the old belt.

Most of us are just as thankful that tomorrow afternoon we will once again partake in that good harvest. And probably partake a few more times over the weekend, say, around kickoff time.

I, for one, will be harvesting two slices of wheat bread with some cold dark meat, lettuce, a little mayo, some salt and a side of mashed potatoes topped with bit of gravy. And probably a side of stuffing with those bits of raisins.

Twist my arm, and I'll even partake in some apple pie.

Yes, on this day of giving thanks, we are very thankful to leave my mother-in-law's house with a bag full of leftover bounty, in containers that will fill my fridge.

Tastes great today, but, come on, don't you think it's better the second time around?

My fellow Americans, it seems I am not alone.

A recent survey for the American Dietetic Association and ConAgra Foods Foundation found that 91 percent of Americans polled said they will be taking home holiday leftovers.

How could we not be thankful for a holiday that actually encourages guests not only to bring their appetites – but their Tupperware.

That's not to say we wake up Thanksgiving morning, eat a hearty breakfast, watch those freckle-faced teens from Mary Poppins High march in their skivvies

Dustin and Daniel with cousins Amy and Emily Hubbert.

to Macy's and around noon whip out a few containers with their equally easily accessible lids.

Maybe in your house.

In our house, if I don't have the container search done by Labor Day, it's a lost cause.

Like the people who work on those floats, we prep all year for this day.

Years ago it was easy. We all started with full sets of Tupperware. Probably got them as a wedding gift. But as the anniversaries start clicking the lids go-a-missing.

These days I spend half my nights playing the mix and match game. Got a container, can't find a lid. Found one lid, but it doesn't fit any container.

I could build a house with all our Cool Whip bowls. But I'd give up a drum stick to find a lid that'll fit just one of these containers.

I know, some of you "borrow" containers from your hosts. Such fools.

Do that and you get home with a spoonful of mashed potatoes in one of those mini-tubs for butter. How long will that last you?

You see, by bringing your own containers, you've enhanced the ability of maximizing your leftover intake.

That's why for a month I have nothing but quarts of wonton soup and lots of margarine.

Don't get me wrong. I love the chance to spend today with family. Pass a biscuit. Swap a tale.

A toast to all. May each and every one have a happy, healthy and hardy Thanksgiving.

And I will do the same. Today. Tomorrow. And if I can come up with just a few more lids – and if no one has seconds – I'll be able to stretch this till Christmas dinner.

November 25, 2004

It's not what's on the inside that counts

Holiday shopping is easy this year.
Everyone is getting a box.
Not a gift in a box. A box as a gift.

I've got no choice. It's the only way the Lewis clan will ever put a dent in our box collection.

Yea, boxes. We hoard boxes like Imelda Marcos hoards shoes.

We've given out gifts, given away gifts, returned gifts, exchanged gifts and at times just threw out gifts.

But the boxes have remained.

In the attic. Piled on top of each other.

A collaboration of corrugated clutter.

In our house, it's not better to give than to receive – it's better that you keep hold of the box you gave and the box you received.

God forbid that you need a box at the last minute and the stores are all out.

Not us.

You see folks, gifts come and go.

They no longer fit. The batteries die. You lose a piece or just lose interest. All that time and effort, all the worry and the money spent, and most of us would be hard-pressed to remember half of what we got last year.

And goshdarn it, no matter how hard you work to find just the perfect gift for that someone special, that someone special is bound to react with, "Oh … that's nice."

But, before they open it and are unable to hide their immense disappointment, they're sincerely dazzled by the box.

"That's a big box!" Or, "Wow, what a box. I can't wait to see the gift."

It's what we call diminished returns.

What did I get last year? What did I give?

Haven't a clue.

Hey, just give me a minute and I'll find you a box that housed a gift. Maybe not last year's gift. Or the year before that. Don't worry. I'll find a box. Because we have boxes.

I'd love to tell you tree huggers out there that the Lewis clan are true green environmentalists, that we recycled to preserve the forest.

I'd love to tell you that.

Truth is, we just don't want to be caught without a box.

In fact we wind up wasting more wrapping paper by trying to cover a box three times the size of the gift.

Freud would suggest that my need to keep boxes goes back to my childhood, when in third grade I had to make a diorama but couldn't find a shoe box.

There've been years that we tried to think outside the box. Use those blue Wal-Mart bags.

But as much as our boxes mean clutter, they also bring back memories, sometimes as much as the gifts they once housed.

Once again we'll pull out the old Currier and Ives holiday box that my wife's grandma gave us more than a dozen years ago. The box is worth more than any gift.

We'll use the box that contained a Hot Wheels car set, which we bought the boys in the late 80s, for the gifts we'll give them this year.

They played with that car set forever.

We threw out the last of the pieces a few years back.

There's a box from Sullivan's in Liberty, from their boutique shop, when I spent more than I could afford on a scarf for my new bride.

And a big box from the Green's store at the Orange Plaza, when my wife decided I needed a special suit.

Both department stores are long gone, but the boxes remain.

There's a shoe box when my son needed cleats and a box that housed our new Betamax. And the sturdy red box that was filled with munchies from close friends.

So this year, we'll tear off the wrapping and toss it in a big black garbage bag. We'll say thanks for the new sweater and put it in the dresser. The holiday nuts will be gone in a week.

But we'll hold on to the boxes, the new ones and the worn ones, carefully bringing them back to the attic until next season.

For us, boxes are the gift that keeps on giving.

December 18, 2003

Barry's Momma Roz

Amid mom's junk lie priceless things

This time it was a 2-foot-high plastic statue of a guy holding a birthday cake, three ceramic planters and a thing to pull out staples.

The time before that it was an old rotary telephone, three used pot holders and a bobble-head hula dancer.

We said no to playing cards with the 10 of hearts missing and a single bookend.

A trip into Brooklyn to see mom wouldn't be complete without leaving with an arm full of dust collectors, a vast array of junk that wouldn't rate space on a yard sale.

Some kids visit their moms and come away with edible delicacies.

Our going away prize may rate a full Kings Plaza Diner carry home bag, but that's only on the outside. Buried in the bag is a wall ornament of dry flowers, cups and bowls of various sizes and colors and a key holder, complete with a useless set of keys.

I understand about the worthless items that she pawns off on us.

It's the revenge of the parent.

For years we thought nothing of living in a pigsty. Our room was our oasis, the ever-growing pile of dirty clothes an offering to the god of shmutz.

Instead of the Meadowlands, here's where they should have been looking for Hoffa.

Of course we saw symmetry in our mess, balanced by a lava lamp in the corner, a Nerf hoop over the closet and the cascading hair and never-ending smile of Farrah sitting just above the bed.

Mom saw a wasteland of filth in a room that deserved to be condemned.

Except for the occasional rhetoric of "so help me…" or the classic "I'm warning you …" she let us be.

I've always wondered why this woman of the cloth – that is wash cloth, dust cloth – allowed such garbage in her house.

Now I get it.

It's garbage payback.

The crap that she managed to collect over the years is being thrown back in my face.

I can understand mom not wanting to keep a half-dozen of those yellow things you snapped into 45s for your record player, a lime green napkin holder and the World Book Encyclopedia yearbooks from 1969 through 1981 (except

1977, still missing in action).

But she won't throw them out.

Instead, they sit in the corner of her apartment, along with an eight-track of Steve and Eydie singing their favorite Jewish dance songs, a recipe book for fondue classics and a salt shaker.

The pile makes the Island of Misfit Toys look like a prized Barbie bin at Christmas.

"You don't want it?"

"Ma, we don't own an eight-track player."

"So, you'll give it to the kids."

It all makes sense.

This is the master plan that was percolating in her head for more than 25 years. Not sure if her grandchildren would be as sloppy as her son, she would plant the seeds of filth by providing us with useless dust collectors.

What better place to house a checkerboard, minus the checkers, than her son's house?

Why toss down the incinerator the centerpiece she won a decade ago from the bar mitzvah of cousin Claire's son Jeffrey, when you can pass it on to your own son?

But with a worn shoe tree came my grandparents' marriage license written in Hebrew and their wedding picture.

I never saw them so young.

They smiled like any newlywed couple, but I swear I could see a twinkle in the eyes of these first-generation Americans, who saw no limits to what they could accomplish together in their new home.

And among her collection of swizzle sticks were all the Mother's Day cards I had given her over the years. She moved a couple of times, but made sure the cards were never left behind.

Now I really understand.

She's not sticking me with junk.

She giving me the treasures of our life, priceless reminders she could not throw away.

Some a bit more valuable than others.

I'll hang up my grandparents' wedding picture. And I'll find a spot for the bobble-head hula dancer. Maybe the boy's room.

March 14, 2002

Sneaker shopping:
It's Mom's choice

My Mom asked us to come down to Brooklyn so we could take her shopping for new sneakers.

Says she wore out her old pair.

I tried to imagine Mom wearing out a pair of sneakers.

She's not what you'd call the athletic type. The last time I could remember her building up a real sweat was when she wiped out our neighbor, Selma, in a hot game of mahjong.

To her a marathon is setting up the VCR to catch three hours of "Judge Young," "Judge Alex" and "Judge Judy" while still managing to catch "The View" and "The Price is Right."

There are many things I can see my mom wearing out. A mop. A dust cloth. A sponge. Sneakers would never make my list.

But she was calling.

There's always an underlying reason for our trips — besides just seeing her. Celebrate a birthday or holiday. Bring down new pictures. Take back old dust collectors she no longer wants but has decided we need.

Our visits don't come soon enough for Mom. She often conveys her frustration in her typical, subtle tone.

"If you can't find the time to see me when I'm alive — don't bother to come see me when I'm dead."

You never have to read between the lines with Mom. So when she suggested we come down because of "sneakers," I was taken aback.

"Are you feeling all right?"

"I'm OK, except for my back. And my chest. And my feet hurt a bit. If I don't walk around or breathe too hard I'll be fine. So, you'll come down and I'll look for sneakers. We'll go to Kings Plaza. I'll buy you fries at Nathan's."

We brought down pictures, she gave us dust collectors she no longer wanted but thought we'd need, and went searching for sneakers.

As we toured Kings Plaza with marathon Mom, I couldn't help but notice the perfect pair of sneakers on her feet.

"What about the pair you're wearing now?"

"They're OK, but, they won't be good in the snow."

"Ma, they're sneakers. You're not supposed to wear them in the snow. You wear snow shoes. Boots."

"What, I'm gonna bother with big boots? Sneakers work in the snow. But they have to be strong."

"So we're looking for strong sneakers that you can wear in snow but aren't as heavy as boots?"

"In white."

"Of course. What else would you wear in snow."

Two hours and seven shops later, Mom finally found the style she was looking for. The fact that they weren't her size didn't seem as important as the amount of heavy leather she perceived to be on the sneaker.

She was ready to try on a pair. She looked around.

"See if they have any Peds," she asked me, sitting in her bare feet."

"Where are your socks?"

"It was hot in the apartment so I didn't want to put anything on."

"But you knew you were shopping for sneakers. Heavy sneakers. Snow sneakers. You're gonna try on sneakers in Peds?"

She did. The heavy sneakers lifted her 3 feet in the air. She was now up to my chin.

Mom showed me the box on the "Cross Trainer 621," and pointed out the shock absorption feature.

"That'll help when you climb the bleachers." I told Jesse Owens to give them a test run.

"They're a bit loose."

"That's because you're not wearing socks and there's no snow in the store. Do you like them?"

"The guy who works here says they can't keep them in stock."

"Ma, the guy gets paid to say they can't keep them in stock. So people like you buy them and then they can't keep them in stock. Do you like them?"

"You think they'll be good in winter?"

"As long as you don't try to outrun the bus they'll be fine. Wear them in the apartment. With socks. If you don't like them, I'll come back down and we'll return them."

"You'll make another trip down?"

"It'll give me another reason to see you."

October 18, 2007

For Mom now, a nod says it all

I look hard into my mom's glassy eyes and hold her weakened hand, colored in black and blue from being used as a medical pincushion.

I steady my voice as I try to assure her she will be fine.

She looks my way and just nods.

It's the nod that turns my eyes into ponds.

I'm 48 and I can remember talking to my mom since I was about 4. At no time in all those years did she ever just nod.

My mom talked. Boy, did she ever talk. Mom could make sailors blush.

There were times I wish she did just nod. Many times.

I couldn't believe the things she said. Out loud. To strangers. To me. About me.

When editors at the Record decided a few years back to interview Roz Lewis for a Mother's Day feature — see if she's really the way I've long described her — they found out the truth.

Then-reporter Kristina Wells got more than a nod when she visited my mom in Brooklyn. She was still upset I hadn't made it down for Passover.

Roz Lewis opens her apartment door and welcomes Kristina:

"Barry's on my &%@ list. Come on in."

That's Roz Lewis.

Never just a nod.

As I stand over her hospital bed, I'm pretty sure she knows who I am, but I don't think she's buying my "you'll be fine" crap.

Only she wouldn't call it crap.

I get a chill just thinking about what must be running through her mind. This is tough.

One day, Roz Lewis is lying on her bed, maybe just to ease a sudden pain in her chest. Next thing, she wakes up tethered to monitors that beep and blink and drip who knows what into her veins.

She can raise her arm and scratch her nose with her left hand, but can't even lift the pinkie finger on her right.

She can see the doctor move her right leg around, but can't feel him move it.

What does it mean that she can't feel her right leg?

Can't feel her right arm?

Can't see out of her right eye? Has trouble remembering?

No more nods from Roz.

She tries to talk, but I can't make out what she's saying.

I tell her she's hard to understand with the oxygen mask.

"It's OK — we'll talk later."

She just nods.

Her doctors tell me they can't believe how alert she is, given the severity of her stroke. They're impressed.

"Your mother must have a strong will."

There's a medical understatement.

I can't tell her what I know.

I can't.

A few weeks ago, I wrote a column that said she'd live to be 100. I remind her of that.

"You gotta get well. You're making me look bad."

She just nods.

I kiss her hand.

She takes mine and brings it to her mouth.

What do I say to a woman who just nods?

I want to tell her that she'll be fine — but I can't.

I squeeze her hand harder.

My brother pulls out a note that his 7-year-old son, Matthew, wrote to his grandma:

Dear Grandma,

I will never forget I love you as hi as the sky. I hope you get this message. We miss you as high as the sky, Grandma!!!

I hope you get out of the hospital real soon, so we can play cards again. I hope you can make me some more frankfurters. I hope me and you can laugh harder and harder when we make double wars. I hope that when we watch tv together in your bedroom, I can lay next to you and eat popcorn and chips.

Make sure you take your inhaler once a day and I hope you can get better real soon.

Love Always

Your grandson

Matthew

She just nods.

April 06, 2008

Right: Roz Lewis with her four-year-old son Barry, 1964.